G000044831

Newnes
Hard Disk
Pocket Book

Newnes Hard Disk Pocket Book

Second edition

Michael Allen and Tim Kay

Newnes
An imprint of Butterworth-Heinemann Ltd
Linacre House, Jordan Hill, Oxford OX2 8DP

 PART OF REED INTERNATIONAL BOOKS

OXFORD LONDON BOSTON
MUNICH NEW DELHI SINGAPORE
SYDNEY TOKYO TORONTO WELLINGTON

First published 1990
Second edition 1992

British Library Cataloguing in Publication Data
A catalogue record for this book is available
from the British Library

ISBN 0 7506 0470 0

Produced by GLM Ltd, 10 Highfields Road,
Mountsorrel, Loughborough, Leicestershire,
England LE12 7HH

Printed in England by Clays Ltd, St Ives plc

Trademarks

Cautionary Note

Dedication

For our parents

Pocket Software Collection

To accompany this book we have assembled a range of software and utilities. For various reasons it is not possible to include this with the book, hence it is available seperately by post. The Collection contains nearly 1 Mb of programs and data and it is available on either 3.5" or 5.25" disk. The Collection costs £6.95 including postage and packing.

To order the disk please write to **BK Software, 4 Britannia House, Station Street, Burton on Trent, Staffs, DE14 1AX** stating which size disk you require, and enclosing a cheque for £6.95 made payable to BK Software.

All orders will be dispatched the same day and BK Software will provide any technical support you require with any of the programs in the Collection.

Contents

Preface

When we wrote the first edition of this book two years ago, we knew that there were major hard disk changes on the way. We could not have foreseen the virtual demise of the ST506 interface and the meteoric rise, even in computer terms, of the IDE interface.

It is just over ten years since IBM launched the first Personal Computer; the event actually occurred on August 11th. 1980. The original machine was a slow, cassette tape based device but it set a new standard for computers. Its biggest attribute was the fact that the computer was purposely left open ended. This meant that it was possible for the purchaser to buy additional bits and pieces and fit them him- or herself and so improve the basic configuration. These days, if you can find an original IBM PC, it will cost you an awful lot of money due to its rarity.

During the years since its release the PC has undergone continuous change and development. It has also been widely copied and duplicated by a host of other companies - some of whom had IBM's blessing and others who did not. Be all that as it may, the PC set a new standard, and that standard continues to exist today.

One of the major advances during this time has been the power and performance of software. There is now more software available for the PC and its related machines, the XT and AT, than any other computer type in the world. However, as the software became more powerful it also got significantly larger. This in turn caused changes in the original machine. First there were floppy disks, single sided and single density, that could hold a maximum of 180 Kb of data.

These were quickly replaced by the 360 Kb double sided floppies, a standard which is still very much in use today, but even these were too small. The software started to arrive on a multitude of disks and the user had the hassle of constantly having to swap disks back and forth, thereby increasing the risk of data damage. Something better than floppies was required.

The answer was hard disks - special motorised units which held a number of fixed disks that provided, by the standards of the time, a colossal amount of storage. Five whole Megabytes! The equivalent of 14 floppies! Nowadays it sounds dreadful but at the time it was a phenomenal step forward. Still the software continued to grow in power and performance and the numbers of floppy disks required for it continued to increase. Newer hard disks appeared, 10 Mb and then 20 Mb. But it became a never ending race as the software continued to increase its capabilities. WordStar 5.0, for example, comes on 17 disks and 6 comes on 24.

New floppies appeared, 5.25-inch 1.2 Mb and then 3.5-inch 1.44 Mb. The 2.88 Megabyte floppy is just starting to appear. Hard disks capacities got larger and larger, and they continue to do so. In 1988 the standard hard disk was 32 Mb. By the end of 1989 the standard had become 70 Mb or more - and the capacity continues to increase. You can even get 1.8 Gigabyte drives ‘off the shelf’ and 2.5 Gigabyte have been field tested.

During 1991 we saw laptop computers fitted with 2.5" hard disks with a capacity of 60 megabytes. One company is working on the next generation of drives for laptops which will be 1.8" drives. They believe that the maximum capacity will be over 200 Megabytes.

Magnetic storage has served the industry well but we are possibly getting close to the limit - after all there are only so many magnetic fields that can be placed onto a disk. There is a limit to how close together they can be packed. So something new was needed. Then Philips invented the CD-Disks. These are slowly being taken up by the computer industry as a means of storing massive amounts of information in a small space - 550 Mb on a 12 cm disk is not to be sneezed at. The big problems with CD technology is that it is not yet possible to read a file, change it and then rewrite it to the disk. Hence they are called CD-ROMs. However they're working on it somewhere and before very long they will solve the problem.

In the meantime we still have the standard magnetic disks. The growth in size and performance has brought its own problems and complications. This book is about solving those problems. It may not solve every one but it will give you sufficient grounding in the basic technology to allow you to use your hard disk effectively, efficiently and correctly.

Because this book is meant to be used as much for reference as for anything else, we have chosen to put the Glossary at the front rather than the back. Given the state of the computer industry, and the fact that is a dynamic, ever evolving beast, it is impossible to write a definitive book about any aspect of it. We have tried to make this as comprehensive as possible, but we are not omnipotent.

Every book is the result of work and effort by a number of people, not just the author. Therefore we would like to take some time here to thank as many of them as possible.

Peter Dixon at Heinemann deserves special thanks because without him there would be no book.

Mike Dalton at Ambar Systems who supplied the latest version of SpeedStor.

Allen Shugart, Brian Ramos and Gary Stapells of Seagate Technologies.

Richard Gray for his patience in the early years.

Alan and Susan Solomens of S&S International.

All our friends and colleagues, too numerous to list separately, in the industry for their help and patience. You know who you are, thanks from both of us.

We hope you will enjoy reading this book as much as we enjoyed writing it. And we are certain that you will find it useful, informative and practical when dealing with your data storage.

M.Allen & T.Kay
December 1991

Glossary

8086 Chip

The microchip from the Intel Corporation which is the heart of many of todays PC's and XT's. The chip possesses a 20-bit address bus, 16-bit data bus and 16-bit registers.

8088 Chip

The junior sister to the above and which was used as the heart of the original PC. This has a 20-bit address bus, only an 8-bit data bus and 16-bit registers. The chip can still be found in many of the lower cost machines available today although it has long since been superseded by faster and more dynamic chips.

80286 Chip

This has a 24-bit address bus, a 16-bit data bus and 16-bit registers. It can operate in both real and protected modes, but cannot be software switched and so cannot be used to run programs concurrently. The chip powers many AT's but it is being replaced by the 80386 as the standard workhorse of such machines.

80386 Chip

The 32-bit address bus, 32-bit data bus and 32-bit registers make this chip the most dynamic currently available in large quantities. It is used to power many AT's and is becoming widely used, to the extent of replacing the 80286 as the standard AT chip. One of its biggest advantages is that it will allow the user to run programs concurrently, i.e. two or more programs at the same time. Unfortunately there is, as yet, very little software available which can take advantage of the dynamism of this chip, although all IBM-compatible software can be run as normal on machines using the 80386.

80386SX Chip
Essentially a cut down version of the previous chip. It has a 24-bit address bus, a 16-bit data bus and 32-bit registers. Like its big sister, the 80386, it can run programs concurrently but it costs much less and so machines based around the chip are less expensive.

80486 Chip
Essentially a fast 80386 with the addition of a built in maths co-processor and a data cache of 8 Kb. It can address 64 Mb of memory. Chips running at 33 Mhz are commonly available and a version running at 50 Mhz is starting to appear.

80486SX Chip
Essentially a cut down version of the previous chip but without the maths co-processor. Like its big sister, the 80486, it can run programs concurrently but it costs much less and so machines based around the chip are less expensive.

80586 Chip
The latest in the 8000 Series family released by the Intel Corporation. At the time of writing there no commercially available computers that use this chip but industry rumours suggest that it will become generally available by mid 1992.

Access Time
The time taken for the information to be found on the disk once you ask the computer to load a particular file or string of data. The time is

usually measured in milliseconds and the faster it is the quicker the computer can manipulate the data. There is a wide range of programs available that will measure the access time for you. Access time becomes especially important when using disk intensive software such as DTP programs or relational databases.

ANSI.SYS

ANSI is an acronym for the American National Standards Institute and it pertains to a set of standard effects that were originally designed in the early days of computers. This command controls the way in which the display, i.e. monitor, produces its effects. It is primarily used by a number of older software packages to create defined colour displays. To use the command it must be included in the CONFIG.SYS file as a device, for example by using the line DEVICE= ANSI.SYS. This means that the command must be in the root directory of the disk that you are booting up your machine from. On a hard disk machine you can modify the line to include the path to the directory that contains the program, e.g. DEVICE=C:\MS-DOS\ANSI.SYS, which allows you to keep your root directory uncluttered. Note that you should always state the full path including the drive designator letter.

Archive Bit

That bit in a file attribute byte that sets the archive attribute. If the bit is set to On, i.e. has a value of 1, then the file is deemed to be new and will be backed up by the MS-DOS BACKUP command. If the bit is Off, value 0, then the file will not be backed up by the command if you use the /M switch. The archive bit is also used by the majority of backup utility programs.

ARLL

Acronym for Advanced Record Length Limited. Another form of RLL recording, it is also called ERLL, the E meaning Enhanced. Not in widespread use.

ASCII

It was decided in the distant past of computing that there should be a recognised standard for all text files so that every one would adopt the same procedure, thus making commands like TYPE work universally. Rather than create a brand new standard it was decided to use an existing one - that which was originally used for the transmission of messages on teletype machines. ASCII stands for the American Standard Code for Information Interchange and it defines a series of unique codes for 128 characters. Thus each individual letter, whether upper or lower case, numerals and certain control codes have a separate code. Later it was decided that 128 characters were not enough and the codes were extended to 255. These are not standardised and so the characters in IBM-Extended ASCII are different from those in the Epson-Extended ASCII character set.

ASCII character

Any 1-byte character from the original ASCII character set. There are only 128 of these because they were originally defined using only 7 bits and this is the maximum number that can be contained in 7 binary digits. The 8th. bit was used for special purposes.

ASSIGN.COM

This external MS-DOS command allows you to 'fool' the computer into believing that one drive is actually another one. Some application software, particularly older ones, requires you to keep data and program files on separate floppy disks - which is fine if you are using a twin floppy machine but can be a nuisance if you have only one floppy drive. (This is one reason for using up to date software by the way.) This command allows you to get round the problem because it forces MS-DOS to treat one drive as another.

Using the command ASSIGN A=B in the batch file which runs the program forces the operating system to ignore the physical presence of Drive-A and always look to Drive-B whenever the application requests the former. All subsequent calls for the disk drives will be affected by the command and so care should be exercised when using it. For instance, there are a number of MS-DOS commands which are 'drive sensitive', e.g. DEL or DIR, and these act on the designated drive - providing that it has not been changed using Assign. Once the assignment has been activated it can be undone very simply by entering the command, at the system prompt, without using any parameters, i.e. ASSIGN, and all the drives will return to their default status.

AT

Abbreviation for Advanced Technology. The third 'generation' personal computer which evolved from the PC and the XT. The most notable features of an AT are:

a) based on an 80286 or 80386 microchip,
b) generally hard disk fitted as standard,
c) high capacity floppy disk drives,
d) 16-bit slots, and
e) the ability to address and use sizable amounts of RAM.

AT's are fast becoming the standard machines used by most businesses, commercial organisations and, although less rapidly, as personal computers. Over the past year they have also become noticeably less expensive until the price difference between an XT and an AT can be as little as £200 - a very small price to pay for the increased performance.

Attribute Byte

A single byte of information that is held in the directory entry of a disk and which relates to a given file. It describes the various attributes of that file. Some of these, such as Read-Only and Archive, can be changed using the ATTRIB command while others can only be altered by utility programs such as PC Tools or Norton Utilities.

ATTRIB.EXE

Each file on your disks, whether it be a system, program or data file, possesses a number of attributes, e.g. the size, date and time of creation, all of which are visible when using DIR. In addition there are four others which you do not normally see and which affect how the file is handled by the operating system. This external MS-DOS command allows you to see and change two of the four, i.e. the Read-Only and the Archive attributes. The other two are Hidden and System but these cannot be seen or set using this command: instead you need to use a utility program like PC Tools or Norton Utilities.

AUTOEXEC.BAT

A batch file that will be executed every time that the computer is booted up, whether cold or warm. It contains a list of programs that you need or want to run every time that the computer is switched on. The file is a pure ASCII one and is very easy to create and/or modify. See also CONFIG.SYS.

Automatic Head Parking

On any disk that has a Voice Coil Actuator the heads will be parked automatically when the power is turned off or otherwise interrupted. This will, hopefully, prevent accidental damage to the disk.

AUX

Refers to an Auxiliary device, specifically the serial port and the device connected to it. The word is one of those reserved by MS-DOS and cannot be used as a filename or as a directory name.

Auxiliary Storage

Any storage device that is not a main storage device, e.g. a tape streamer.

Average Latency

The time that is taken for any single byte of information to reach the Read/Write Heads of the disk. Normally this is 30% of the time taken for the disk to rotate.

Average Seek Time

The time taken for the Read/Write Heads to move from one track to another. A number of utility programs will provide this information for you accurately, e.g. SpinRite - some manufacturers' estimates tend to be prone to a little exaggeration.

Backup

1) The process of making a duplicate copy of a file on another disk so as to protect yourself from

its loss in case of damage to the original disk. Backups can be something as simple as copying the file to another disk, using the BACKUP command, or any purpose written program that will do this for you.

2) The disk, normally a floppy, that contains the backup copies of files.

3) The MS-DOS external command which is used to create contingency copies of files so that data loss as a result of a disk head crash is minimised. To be of any real use the command must be used regularly. The files backed up can only be replaced using the RESTORE command.

Bad Sector
Any sector of the disk that has been damaged, from whatever cause, and so cannot be used for storing information. As a disk gets older it is likely to develop more bad sectors as the magnetic coating becomes worn. Some utility programs can 'repair' bad sectors and restore them to active use.

BAS
A reserved word used as the extension to BASIC program files and which cannot therefore be used for naming files or directories.

BASIC
An acronym for Beginner's All Purpose Symbolic Instruction Code. A programming language that is probably the most common on personal computers. It is typified by using commands which are close to common English and thus it is 'easy' to learn and understand. There are many varieties of BASIC available and they are not

fully compatible but they all share the same common format.

BAT
The file extension given to Batch files and as such this is a word that is reserved by MS-DOS for its own purposes.

Batch File
Any pure ASCII file created by the user that is used to run a series of commands. Batch files can be extremely powerful in their effects but they are simple to construct. All batch files must have the extension BAT - which is also a reserved word.

Bay
An opening in the computer case that gives access to the carrier and is used to hold the various drives that form the main storage devices.

Bezel
The front cover that masks the face of the disk drive and which helps to prevent dirt and dust getting into the machine. Normally made of impact resistant plastic and containing an indicator light.

Binary
A mathematical system which uses Base 2, thus the only two digits it allows are 0 and 1. Any denary number can be written in binary but they tend to get rather long. It is generally supposed that computers work using binary, with 0 representing a switch being Off and the 1 representing the opposite although in reality, binary is used by humans to notate the working of the machine.

BIOS

Acronym for Basic Input/Output System. The BIOS is part of the operating system that handles how the computer communicates with the outside world through its peripherals. Generally the BIOS is part of the ROM and hence unchangeable.

BIT

An abbreviation of Binary digIT. It represents a single binary number, either 0 or 1. A collection of Bits, normally eight, is called a Byte and this is the minimum space required to hold a single character. This forms the basis for most operations within the computer.

Boot

To load any program into the computer. More usually, as in boot up the computer, it means turning on the power so the machine performs the POST and then loads the operating system. A boot operation in this instance may be either cold, i.e. switching the whole machine on after it has been off for some time, or warm, i.e. pressing Ctrl-Alt-Del. Both methods load or reload the operating system.

Boot Record

A one-sector record which is on every disk that informs the operating system about the disk concerned and the files it contains. The boot record is always the very first sector on a disk and hence it is the one most likely to be damaged. Any disk without a boot sector cannot be used and will produce an error message. Equally if the boot sector is damaged then the disk becomes unusable. Occasionally, reformatting can repair the damage but any data held on the disk will be lost as a result.

Buffer

A predefined area of the computer memory in the RAM, that is used as temporary storage to hold data before it is transferred from the application to the disk. The number of buffers to be used is set in the CONFIG.SYS file although there is a certain minimum that you must use.

Byte

A 'word' of eight bits which is the minimum amount of space necessary to hold a single character, e.g. the upper case letter A is ASCII denary code 65 which can be written in binary as 01000001, this latter being the byte. Note that a byte can also be 16 or 32 bits.

Carrier

The framework, normally steel, to which the drive units are attached by small screws and which is accessed via the bay. On some machines the carrier itself is removable.

Cassettes

Magnetic tape attached to two reels which are contained in a plastic case. The cassette can be used as serial data storage.

CD-Disk

A 12 cm diameter plastic disk that is coated with aluminium onto which a laser can imprint data. Originally used for music publishing, the disks can also be used for publishing volumes of data compactly and efficiently. The storage capacity is vast and the majority of CD-Disks currently available can hold a minimum of 550 Megabytes.

CD-ROM
An optical storage device which is used to hold large quantities of unchanging data. Unfortunately the disks can normally only be read from and not written to - hence the name ROM.

CHDIR or CD
Abbreviation for Change Directory. The internal MS-DOS command that allows you to log onto different directories on the disk.

Chip
A contraction of Microchip - another name for the integrated circuit. Chip is the generic name applied to the wafer of silicon, which has been 'doped' with impurities, onto which minute components are etched during manufacture. Secured to a ceramic or plastic carrier, the chips form the basis of any modern computer.

CHKDSK
An MS-DOS internal utility program that allows you, at its most superficial level, to examine the files on the disk and check them for contiguity. The command can also be used to perform a low intensity test of the entire disk. Short for Check Disk.

Clean Room
A specially ventilated, dust and contaminant-free environment. Used for manufacturing microchips and also for building and/or servicing hard disk drives. Generally speaking such areas will have less than 100 particles of dust, all less than 0.5 microns, per cubic foot of space. They cost a fortune to construct and maintain. A hard disk should never be opened, or the platters exposed, other than in such an environment.

Clock
A thin wafer of quartz usually embedded in a tin alloy. This can be made to vibrate by applying an electrical current to it. The resulting oscillations can then be monitored and used as a highly accurate timing device. All computer operations are then synchronised by this clock.

Clone
Any machine which emulates the IBM standard but not completely. It will contain minor differences and foibles and is thus not 100% identical. Compare Compatible.

CLS
An internal MS-DOS command which clears the monitor screen and then displays the system prompt, most often used in batch files. The letter combination cannot be used for naming files or directories as it is a command name.

Cluster
A group of sectors that is the minimum amount of storage space that the computer can allocate and use. The number of sectors per cluster depends on the type of disk being used.

COM
A reserved word. Refers to the Communications port and is also used as the extension to certain programs.

COMMAND.COM
An operating system file, the third such to be loaded when the computer is booted up, that provides the user interface and the internal commands.

Compatible
Any machine that is a near perfect copy of the standard IBM computer. The machines will be almost identical and therefore there will be no compatibility problems with them when running identical software. Compare Clone.

Computer
A collection of electronic and mechano-electrical devices housed in a steel or plastic box which is capable of performing repetitive tasks at an incredible rate, far faster than the human brain. An electronic idiot savant.

CON
Refers to the keyboard and/or the monitor and is an abbreviation for Console. As such it is a reserved word and cannot be used for naming files.

CONFIG.SYS
A pure ASCII file that contains details of the user preferences that will apply to the computer's operation.

Console
A hangover from the early days of computers, which referred to the input and output device - usually a typewriter or teleprinter - monitors being unheard of. The word is occasionally used today to refer to the keyboard and/or monitor.

Contiguous
Simply put, it means touching. When used to refer to files it means that these are all stored in adjoining sectors on the disk, instead of being stored in random locations. Any file placed on to a new disk will automatically be contiguous

but as the file is modified and moved back and forth it will tend to become scattered throughout the entire disk, even to the extent of being on separate platters. There are a number of utility programs, e.g PC Tools Compress or Norton Speed Disk, that will make all files contiguous and thereby speed up the file access time.

Controller

The collection of electronic components that manage the interaction of a physical device, i.e. a hard disk, with the computer. It can be built into the device as in a Hard Card, or it can be on a separate board that must be connected to the device as with a hard disk.

Cookies

The name applied to the discs of plastic which will, after further processing, become floppy disks.

Crash

Anything that causes the computer to hang up, e.g. an interruption of the power supply or a fault in a program. In the event of a disk crash some data files may be corrupted to a greater or lesser extent and may be scattered all over the storage device(s). Fortunately crashes do not occur very often but they are one reason for making sure that you always backup important data.

Cursor

Normally a thin flashing line that shows the position at which whatever you type on the keyboard will appear. The cursor shape can be changed as a result of running some software. Also, mistakenly, called the prompt.

Cylinder

The name given to the tracks on a hard disk and, less often, on a floppy disk. So called because the tracks are 'stacked' above each other and essentially form a cylinder. Data can be read from anywhere within that series of tracks without having to move the Read/Write heads.

Daisy Chain

Daisy chaining is a method of having two or more devices use the same interface on the one controller. On hard disks, daisy chaining is done only with the control lines, e.g. on an ST 506 interface this is the 34 way cable. The data lines are never daisy chained but each device has its own data cable.

Data

Any collection of facts or information.

Data Cable

1) On a floppy disk it is the ribbon cable, normally with 34 wires, which carries the data and control signals to and from the drive and the computer.

2) On a hard disk using the ST 506/412 interface it is the ribbon cable, normally with 20 wires, which carries the data from the computer to the drive. There is also a second cable, containing 34 wires, which carries the control signals.

3) On SCSI hard disks it is a single cable, containing 64 wires, which carries both the data and control signals.

Data Transfer Rate

The speed at which data is read from the disk and transferred to another device.

Defragment
The process, usually carried out by a special utility program, that rearranges a file on the disk so that it is contiguous instead of being scattered.

Default
Any non-specified assumption. For example, entering DIR will give you a listing of files in the directory of the drive you are logged onto - the default drive and directory.

Denary
The standard system of mathematics and counting that we all learn, i.e. Base 10, which has ten digits. Compare Binary and Hex.

Density
The amount of information that can be packed onto a given area of any disk.

Device Driver
A special program that controls, and thereby allows you to use, a non-standard device, e.g. a ramdrive. The device must be named in the CONFIG.SYS for it to be operable.

Diagnostics
A suite of programs that allow the user to investigate, and sometimes cure, problems on the storage media.

DIR
An MS-DOS internal command that allows you to see what files are stored on the current drive and/or directory. By adding additional parameters to the command it is possible to examine any connected disk or directory.

Directory
An area of any disk that is used to contain files. Every disk contains at least one directory, the Root, but this can be divided into sub-directories which are then used to hold related files and/or programs.

Directory Entry
The record, held in the root directory, that relates to any file or sub-directory and which allows the operating system to know about that file or directory. The entry includes the name, size, time and date and stamping, starting cluster and other related information about the file or directory.

Disk
A disc of plastic or metal which bears a coating that can be magnetised in a specific pattern and thus used to store data. The word should always be spelled with a 'k' because it is a contraction of diskette.

Disk Drive
The electro-mechanical device that is used to read from and/or write to disks. The drive unit contains motors, heads, a spindle and other parts that allow the disk to be spun at speed, so that the computer can access the data the disk contains.

EEPROM
Acronym for Electronically Erasable Programmable Read Only Memory. This is similar to an EPROM except that it can be erased by using an electric current. In most AT's certain information about the computer, e.g. the number of disk drives, graphics adaptor, etc., will be stored on an EEPROM - often referred to as the CMOS RAM.

EnDec

Acronym for Encoder Decoder. It refers to the device on the controller that converts the data to and from electrical signals from the computer or magnetic signals from the disk. The actual encoding/decoding takes place on the controller card and is analogous to using a modem to translate signals.

EPROM

An acronym for Erasable Programmable Read-Only Memory. Such devices are normally a special kind of microchip used to store unchanging data. The chips can be erased only by exposure to certain frequencies of ultraviolet light.

Error Message

Any notification, generally displayed on the monitor screen, which informs the user that something is wrong, e.g. a command may have been input incorrectly.

EXE

A reserved word. Used as the extension to Executable files. Must not be used for naming files or as an extension.

External Command

Any MS-DOS command which is not part of the COMMAND.COM and which must, therefore, be stored and accessible before it can be used. The accessibility can be created by using the PATH command.

FAT

Acronym for File Allocation Table. A special area of all disks, held near the outer edge of the disk, that tells the operating system which sectors are allocated to each file and where such sectors are to be located.

FDISK
The MS-DOS program which is used to identify the hard disk to the operating system and then divide the disk into partitions. Normally the command is only run once, as it will destroy any data contained on the disk.

File
An assembly of information/data that is stored as a single unit. Files can be purely data based, e.g. produced by a word processor or database, or they can be program based and store the coding of the program.

FILES
A command in the CONFIG.SYS file which specifies the number of files that the operating system can have open at any one time.

File Attribute
Any of the four 'switches' which relate to a file and cause it to be treated in certain ways.

Filename
The 'word' of up to eight characters which is used to label any file. Certain characters and words are not permissible and are treated by the operating system as Reserved Words. Filenames can also have an extension of up to three characters but this is not essential.

File Recovery
The process of reassembling a file which has been damaged for whatever reason - usually performed by a utility program.

Fixed Disk

Another name for Hard Disk.

Floppy Disk

A thin layer of Mylar coated with material which can be magnetically induced to store information in a form accessible by the computer. The term is descriptive because the disks are not rigid.

FORMAT.EXE

An MS-DOS external command that is used to lay down a pattern of magnetism on a floppy or hard disk so that the disk can be used by the computer operating system to store files. Using the command will destroy any data that the disk contains.

Formatted Capacity

The measure of the total storage capacity of a disk, usually measured in Kilobytes on a floppy disk or in Megabytes on a hard disk, once it has been formatted.

Front End

Any program which appears on the screen as the default in place of the prompt.

Gigabyte

A huge amount of data space, either on a disk or referring to the computer's RAM, abbreviated to Gb. A Giga is a multiplier which is indicative of 1 Billion (1,000,000,000) of something. In actuality, because computers work using the Binary system, 1 Gigabyte is 1,073,741,824 or 2^{30} bytes. Compare Kilobyte, Megabyte and Terabyte.

Hard Card

A hard disk which is secured to an expansion board which also contains the Controller, and can be placed into one of the available expansion slots of the computer. They are characterised by not requiring an independent power supply or any additional cables. Normally only used on PC's or XT's.

Hard Disk

A collection of aluminium platters that are connected together as a single unit and which are then used to store files and data. Hard disk drives fit into one of the vacant slots at the front of the computer. They are characterised by requiring an independent power supply, i.e. a separate lead which runs from the computer's internal power supply, a controller card and two cables in order to work. Hard disks come is a range of different capacities, from 20 Mb to the largest commercially available of around 720 Mb.

Hardware

The collection of physical equipment that makes up the computer system. Compare Software.

HDA

Acronym for Hard Disk Assembly. The HDA is the sealed chamber which contains the platters and Read/Write Heads and which should never be opened except in a clean room.

Head Actuator

The device that moves the Read/Write Heads across the disks surface so that it can locate data. See also Stepper Motor and Voice Coil Actuator.

Head Crash

A calamitous but rare occurrence when the Read/Write Heads literally crash into the surface of the disk and damage the magnetic coating.

Hexadecimal

A numbering system that uses Base 16, i.e. it has sixteen digits. Hexadecimal is much used in relation to computers because it allows large numbers to be presented in very few digits. The system is not as complex as many people suppose - anyone who can use the imperial weight measures, i.e. lbs. and ounces, uses this system. For example 17 ozs. would be written as 1 lb 1 oz, in HEX this would be 11 - i.e. (1*16) plus (1*1). Compare Binary and Denary.

High Level Format

The formatting performed by the MS-DOS FORMAT command on either a floppy or hard disk. It automatically creates the Root directory and the File Allocation Tables on any disk which is so treated.

Interface

The device or 'protocol' that will allow one device to communicate with another, e.g. the parallel interface which allows communication with a printer.

Interleave

The method of numbering the sectors of a disk, so that the next wanted sector moves under the Read/Write Heads at the same time as the computer is ready to access the data that the sector contains.

Interleave Factor
The number of sectors which move past the Read/Write Heads between one sector access and the next. The factor is expressed as a ratio, e.g. 4:1. This means that the first sector is read, then three pass the heads before the next is read and so on, i.e. every fourth sector is read.

Internal Command
Any MS-DOS command which is part of the COMMAND.COM and can be used without having to have the command stored and accessible on the disk.

Jumper
A small piece of plastic which contains contacts that fit over a pair of pins on a circuit board and so forms a conductive path between them.

Kilo
The designation for 1,000 as in kilometres, i.e. 1,000 metres. In computer related terms the number is 1,024 because it is based in binary and is 2^{10}.

Kilobyte
1,024 bytes. Usually abbreviated to Kb and used as a measure of the capacity of a disk or the computer's RAM. With today's machines the word is being superseded by Megabytes.

Landing Zone
The unused track on the disk where the Read/ Write Heads can be safely placed when the power is turned off. Also called the Parking Zone. It is used to prevent accidental head crashes which would damage the disk surface.

Logical Drive

Normally this is any drive named by MS-DOS as the drive specifier, e.g. A:, B: or C:. It is now possible to have a physical drive which contains a number of logical drives as in the case of very large capacity drives. Also known as a Partition.

Lost Clusters

Any number of clusters which for some reason have been recorded in the FAT as being unavailable because they belong to a file. In fact they do not and they can therefore be used for storage. You can recover lost clusters using the CHKDSK command but the facility in Norton Disk Doctor is much better and fully automatic.

Low Level Format

The formatting process that divides the tracks into sectors. It produces sector and track information which is normally unchangeable.

LPT

An abbreviation for Line Printer. It is one of the reserved words and thus cannot be used for naming files or directories.

Magnetic Domain

A very small section of a track that is just large enough to contain a magnetic flux reversal which is used to encode the data on a disk.

Magneto-Optical Recording

A form of Optical Storage which uses the beam from the laser to heat the disk surface allowing the magnetic head to change the magnetic flux. Thus it allows the data to be changed.

Master Boot Record

A single sector on a hard disk that holds essential information about the disk so that the operating system can use it. It also contains the information about the partitions. This sector is always the first one on the disk which is why if it is damaged, your entire disk can become inaccessible.

Mega

A multiplier that refers to 1,000,000 as in the term Megohms which refers to One Million Ohms, or Megawatts which means One Million Watts.

Megabyte

Not 1,000,000 bytes but, because it is 2^{20}, actually 1,048,576 bytes. Used as a measure of a computer's memory and also to measure the capacity of disks. Compare Kilobyte, Gigabyte and Terabyte.

Memory Resident Program

Any program which, once loaded, resides in the computer's memory. It can then be activated at any time by pressing a combination of keys. It is not a good idea to have a number of such programs loaded at the same time and in certain cases they can be detrimental. Also called TSR programs.

Menu

Any program that presents you with a graphical or semi-graphic front end screen which will allow you to activate other programs without having to use the standard operation method, i.e. enter commands from the keyboard to the system prompt.

MFM
Acronym for Modified Frequency Modulation.

Microsecond
One millionth of a second, i.e. 0.000001 of a second.

Millisecond
One thousandth of a second, i.e. 0.001 of a second, normally abbreviated to ms - always lower case.

MKDIR or MD
Abbreviation for Make Directory. The MS-DOS internal command that allows you to create directories and sub-directories.

Modified Frequency Modulation
Usually abbreviated to MFM. It is a method of encoding data so that it can be written onto the surface of the disk. It is also used to specify that each track will have 17 sectors. One of the two standard controllers used for hard disks. Compare RLL.

MS-DOS
Acronym for Microsoft Disk Operating System. Probably the most widely used operating system in the world. MS-DOS is only made available to OEM's and cannot be bought over the counter by end users.

Mylar
Dupont's brand name for a special non-woven polyester which is used for making floppy disks. Characterised by the ability to resist tearing in any direction until the surface is cut.

Nanosecond

One billionth of a second, i.e. 0.000000001 of a second. Normally abbreviated to ns - note the lower case.

Network

Any collection of computers and/or workstations which are connected together so that they form a single entity. Normally there will be a base machine, the Server, which holds all the data and program files as well as being connected to the output devices. The work stations are also called Nodes.

Nodes

The name applied to the computers or workstations which are part of a network but are not the Server.

Norton Utilities

A suite of utility programs that are almost essential if you use a hard disk. Highly recommended - considered essential.

OEM

Acronym for Original Equipment Manufacturer. The term refers to any company which manufactures original equipment (logically enough) but anyone who makes computers, whether clones or compatibles, or peripheral devices can be an OEM.

Operating System

The collection of programs which allow the computer to operate. It performs the essential housekeeping tasks that the system requires. The best known example of such a system is MS-DOS.

Optical Disk

The data storage medium of the next decade? An aluminium disk, coated with a microfine layer of gold, which is used to store immense amounts of data in a very small space. The disks, CD-ROMS, need to be read by a laser because that is the only thing which can be tuned sufficiently finely to allow it to access the microscopic pits of the disk surface.

Park

To position the Read/Write Heads of a hard disk in a location, normally an unused track, such that the likelihood of them hitting the platters and so damaging the stored data is minimised. The heads should always be parked if you intend moving the computer, even if it is only from one desk to another.

Park Program

A special program, normally supplied with the hard disk, that will park the heads. The best park programs require you to reboot the machine completely to unpark the heads.

Partition

The division of a hard disk in separate logical drives to which individual drive designator letters can be applied, created by the FDISK program.

PATH

An internal MS-DOS command that allows you to specify a number of directories and sub-directories so that the programs they contain can be accessed from anywhere on the disk.

PC

Acronym for Personal Computer. The original IBM PC was launched on August 11th. 1980, although there had been a number of computers which deserved the name PC before this - including one from IBM themselves. Today a PC is characterised by having an 8088 or 8086 microchip and no hard disk. Compare AT and XT.

PC Tools

A suite of utility programs which provide a host of facilities for making disk management easier. Essential if you are using a hard disk.

Peripheral

Any device or piece of equipment which is attached to the computer system, e.g. a printer, disk drive, keyboard, etc.

Physical Drive

The actual disk drive, either floppy or hard, which is fitted into the computer. The operating system then defines the logical drives and gives each one a distinct name, e.g. A:, B:, etc. A physical drive may contain a number of partitions which are treated as separate logical drives.

Platters

A disc of aluminium, coated with material onto which a pattern of magnetism can be induced. Within a hard disk drive there will be a number of these arranged one above the other. Data can be stored on both sides of the platter.

Port

A socket into which another device can be connected so that it can communicate with the computer.

POST

Acronym for Power On Self Test. The series of diagnostic tests that the computer automatically runs every time the machine is booted.

Power Line

The four-part cable with pin connectors that runs from the computer power supply to the disk drive. It supplies power at the correct amperage and voltage.

Primary Partition

The first partition of a disk, i.e. the one in which the operating system is stored and from where it is activated whenever the computer is turned on.

PRN

Abbreviation for Printer. A reserved word that cannot be used for naming files or directories.

Program

A set of instructions which performs specific tasks, e.g. a word processor, a financial system or a database. Always spelled with a single 'm' to distinguish the word from programme.

PROM

Acronym for Programmable Read Only Memory. A type of memory chip which contains unchanging and unchangeable information such as an operating system.

PROMPT

An MS-DOS internal command that can have numerous parameters applied to it which allow you to vary how the system prompt appears and which can force it to perform other functions.

RAM

Acronym for Random Access Memory. Refers to the actual memory that the computer uses for storing and manipulating data. RAM is ephemeral and as such any interruption of the power supply will destroy its contents. Compare ROM.

RAM Disk

A pseudo-disk which is actually part of the computer's RAM. It can be treated as a real drive, i.e. to store files, create directories, etc., but it is only present while the computer has power. Any interruption of the power and the contents of the RAM Disk will be lost.

Read/Write Heads

The physically existing heads that move together as a unit between the platters of a hard disk or on either side of a floppy disk and which read or write data. The movement of the heads is controlled by the Actuator Motor.

Reserved Words

Certain words and characters cannot be used for naming files and/or directories because they have a special meaning to the operating system. The forbidden words are AUX, BAT, BAS, COM, CON, EXE, LPT, PRN and SYS. In addition you cannot use the following characters anywhere in the name when labelling files or directories: “ $ * + = [ ] : ; | \ <, >. ? a blank space, or any control codes.

RLL

Acronym for Run Length Limited encoding. One of the two popular controller systems for hard disks, the other being MFM. RLL encoding is considered to be more efficient and faster than

MFM and it gets a lot more data (up to 50% more) onto the equivalent disk - but it can cause other problems which can negate its greater abilities.

RMDIR or RD

Abbreviation for Remove Directory. Directories, although files, are special ones and cannot be deleted using the DEL command. If you use DEL [directory] then you will delete all the files in the directory but not remove the directory itself - except when running Windows, which is a special case. To remove the directory you must use RD [directory].

ROM

Acronym for Read Only Memory. A special memory microchip into which the information is burned in so that it cannot be changed or altered.

Root Directory

The main directory of any disk which is created as the disk is formatted. It is a fixed size and it can hold a maximum of 512 files and/or first level directories.

SCSI

Acronym for Small Computer System Interface. It allows a number of devices to communicate with each other efficiently. Previously used by Apple, it is becoming a standard for IBM-Compatible machines, most notably with Optical Drives.

Sector

As the disk is being formatted the operating system lays down a series of concentric tracks. These are then further divided into 'pie slices' - the sectors. The number of sectors depends on the type of disk involved, e.g. a floppy may have 9 sectors. Each sector can hold a maximum of 512 bytes of data. When the operating system allocates disk space to any file it is always determined in terms of clusters, which are multiples of sectors. Again, the number depends on the type of disk involved.

Software
The generic name for computer programs and data files. Compare Hardware.

Spindle
The post within a disk drive onto which the platters are mounted. In the case of a floppy disk the term refers to the axle which spins the disk.

SpinRite
A utility program which is capable of reformatting the hard disk without the user first having to remove the data such a disk contains. It also provides a host of other facilities such as being able to change the interleaving of the disk. Consider it essential.

ST-506/412
The standard interface which is used by the vast majority of hard disk drives in IBM-compatible computers. Created by Seagate Technologies and introduced in 1980 it has been the standard interface ever since. However over the next couple of years it will possibly disappear and be replaced by SCSI.

Stepper Motor Actuator
An assembly which moves the Read/Write Heads across the platters by means of small partial turns of the stepper motor.

Sub-Directory
A special kind of file into which other files can be stored, or within which other directories can be created. Created using the MD command.

SYS
A reserved word which cannot be used for naming files or directories.

System Crash
A complete breakdown of the computer system which necessitates rebooting the machine from scratch. All work in progress will be lost and the associated disk files may be corrupted. Occasionally a system crash will be fatal, requiring you to engage the services of a repair engineer.

System Prompt
The combination of drive designator and prompt which appears on the monitor whenever you boot up the system. The point at which anything typed on the keyboard will appear. It may be modified using the PROMPT command.

Tera
A multiplier that refers to One Trillion, i.e. 1,000,000,000,000, of something.

Terabyte
Not 1,000,000,000,000 bytes but, because it is 2^{40}, 1,099,511,627,776 bytes. As yet the term is relatively uncommon, but within five years it is likely to be as commonplace as Megabyte, especially in terms of data storage capacities. Compare Kilobyte, Gigabyte and Megabyte.

TPI

Acronym for Tracks Per Inch. A measure of the density of the tracks on any disk. 360 Kb disks have 48 TPI whereas 1.2 Mb disks have 96 TPI. All 3.5-inch disks have 135 DPI.

Track

One of the concentric circles laid down on a disk as part of the formatting process. The tracks are then divided into sectors which are allocated as clusters and this forms the basis of all magnetic data storage. The outer tracks are, of necessity, larger than the inner ones but each will be divided into the same number of sectors, regardless of the size. A single track on MFM hard disks will hold a maximum of 8.5 Kb of data. On RLL drives the figure can be 13 Kb.

Track to Track Seek Time

The length of time taken for the Read/Write Heads to move from one track to another picked at random, usually measured in milliseconds.

TSR

Acronym for Terminate and Stay Resident. Another name for Memory Resident Program.

TYPE

The internal MS-DOS command that will allow you to display ASCII files on screen and read them. You can also TYPE program files but all you get is junk characters and strange noises.

Unformatted Capacity

The measure of the total number of bytes of data that could be placed onto the unformatted disk. The formatted capacity is always lower because space is lost in defining the sectors.

Utility Program

Any program that makes using the computer or disk drives easier and more manageable. The best known are Norton Utilities, PC Tools and SpinRite - three programs the authors consider essential.

Virtual Disk

Another name for RAM Disk.

Voice Coil Actuator

A device that moves the Read/Write Heads across and between the platters of a hard disk by inducing magnetism in coils of wire. The name originated with audio speaker technology.

Volume

Any portion of the disk, i.e. a partition, which is treated as a single logical drive and as such has its own designator, e.g. C:, D: or K:, and to which a separate label or name can be applied. Floppy disks are treated as individual volumes and only the drive is given a designator letter.

Volume Label

The name, which can be up to 11 characters excepting the reserved words and characters, applied to a partition or floppy disk.

Windows

The operating system shell that uses Windows, Icons, Mouse and Pull-down menus instead of the bare system prompt. Windows is, arguably, the most impotant software development in recent times and it will continue to affect all software production for the next five years - if not longer.

Winchester Drive

Another name for a hard disk drive. So called because the originals were developed in Winchester, U.S.A.

Worm Drive

Acronym for Write Once, Read Many times. Also called a CD-ROM.

XT

Acronym for eXtended Technology. The term refers to a standard PC to which a hard disk has been fitted.

Chapter 1 History of Computers

Introduction

Today's personal computers are an entirely different breed to the original launched by IBM in August 1980. They are faster, more powerful, more dynamic and as a result more complex. However, the basic 'genus' remains the same. All personal computers, by which we mean IBM machines, the compatibles and clones, are based around the Intel Corporation 8000 series microchips and they use MS-DOS as their standard operating system. Yes, we know about the Apple, Atari and Commodore machines - but they are so different that they need to be treated separately, although it has to be said that much of what will appear in this book is equally applicable to the disk drives fitted to them as well.

Any computer system is based around the same basic components: the system box, which contains the micro-processor, memory, expansion slots, ports and a means of storing and retrieving information. The keyboard and monitor form the 'console'; i.e. a means of input and a visible means of output.

This book, as it's name suggests will concentrate on the storage devices call 'Hard Disk Drives'. However before we do that, let's take a brief look at the basic IBM PC, its clones and its history.

The original IBM machine was based around the Intel 8088 microchip running at 4.77 Mhz and included the BASIC programming language as standard. It had 16 Kb of memory which was expandable to 64 Kb. For data storage the original machine used standard cassette tapes, i.e. it had only serial storage capabilities. However, within weeks of the launch, this was found to be insufficient and so the machines were then fitted with a single 160 Kb floppy disk drive. This drive used only one side of the disk, which theoretically couldn't be turned over. Although some ingenious souls did make a little device to allow this to be done, more of this later. It had five expansion slots, two of which were used by the system for the monitor output and the floppy drive interface. The remaining three were available for other add-ons. The operating system it used was MS-DOS, although it was relabelled PC-DOS.

MS-DOS is a story unto itself. Originally IBM wanted to use the standard operating system of the time, CP/M, but this wasn't powerful enough to use with the new 16-bit chips. They approached Digital Research to get an updated version, CP/M 16, but for some reason DR were uninterested and so Big Blue had to look elsewhere.

In the meantime there was a little company in Seattle called Seattle Computer Products. They had developed a 16-bit operating system some time earlier but they couldn't find anyone who wanted it. Developing new standards costs money and so they ended up selling the operating system, the complete copyright and all future development rights, to another company called Microsoft. At that time Microsoft was known for producing programming languages and very little else. But they took the infant operating system, called Q-DOS, (rumoured to stand for Quick & Dirty Operating System!), revamped and improved it and called it MS-DOS - Microsoft Disk Operating System.

They approached IBM or vice versa, because nobody now seems too sure about the actual sequence of events, who decided that MS-DOS was exactly what they were looking for. They therefore used it as the standard operating system for their new PC. As a result, Microsoft has gone on to become one of the largest software companies in the world. MS-DOS is supplied with every personal computer that IBM manufacture, and is also supplied with every clone and compatible made by everyone else.

One of its main attractions is its portability; it will run on any 8000 series processor based machine, and although some manufacturers have slightly modified it to take advantage of certain design features of their particular machine, it is the same MS-DOS whether it comes on a genuine IBM or a Joe Bloggs Clone.

Anyway let's get back to the machines! The original Personal Computer was sold, with minor variations in specification, for five and a half years - an enormous period of time in computer terms. But by the time it was withdrawn it was totally obsolete when compared to the newer and later machines.

Its legacy was the term 'Personal Computer', i.e. initialled like this, 'PC' and has, by common usage, come to mean any machine which is based around the 8000 series of microprocessors which use MS-DOS as a base operating system. Yes, we also know about UNIX, XENIX, NOVELL, PICK and PC-BOSS, in fact there are several other operating systems in use, but the one thing they all have in common is that if the processor is an 8000 series, then it will run MS-DOS.

The next evolutionary step was the XT, which stands for eXtended Technology. This was, and still is, a standard PC to which a hard disk drive has been added, in addition to a single floppy drive. Apart from the Hard Disk there is little or no difference between a PC and an XT.

The next step, and a major one, is the AT. The letters stand for Advanced Technology. The first AT's were based around the 80286 microchip but they also had other significant differences. An AT will have the following features:

An 80286 microchip.
A hard disk as standard, plus floppy drive(s)
A minimum of 1 Mb of RAM, expandable to at least 8 Mb.
High capacity floppy drive(s).
Can work in Real or Protected mode but cannot be software switched.
Has 16-bit expansion slots.
A real time clock.

It has one very important feature. It is downwards compatible. This means that it will run any software that was originally written for an original PC using the same operating system.

This downwards compatibility is both the strength and the weakness of all PC systems. Because the chips, which are the important element, can operate in the same way as their predecessors there is no problem with changing software. But this is also the limiting factor. There are other chips available, e.g. the Motorola 68000 Series, which are much faster and more dynamic, but neither IBM nor any compatible manufacturer can switch to these better chips or they will lose this one very important feature.

The evolution continued. The next chip in the series was the 80386, after this came the 80486.The 80386 differed from the 80286 mainly in that the whole architecture of the chip was designed to be 32 bits wide. For a long time these were very expensive and so they only appeared in prestigious machines that cost large sums of money. However they have gradually become much cheaper, thanks to the economies of scale, and you can now buy a 80386 based machine for very little more than an 80286 based machine cost 18 months ago. For some strange reason these machines were not given a separate distinguishing label but were lumped in with the AT's.

In late 1990 the 80486 chip was released in commercial quantities and is now widely available. In essence the 80486 is basically a fast 80386 but with one major difference, a maths co-processor is built in to the chip as is an 8 Kb data cache. As we write, an 80486 based machine running at a clock speed of 33 Mhz is commonly being sold at similar prices to those of an 80386 25 Mhz system of a year ago!

The features common to the high powered AT's are:

80386 or 80486 microchip.
Hard disk as standard.
At least 2 Mb, more usually 4 Mb, of RAM expandable to 4 Gigabytes.
High capacity drives.
Real, Protected and Virtual Real modes of operation, which are software switchable.
16 bit and 32-bit expansion slots.
A real-time clock.

The machines use the AT serial port interface and the same kind of memory. Again it retains its downwards compatibility. Within the AT grouping itself there are also minor differences, like Memory Wait States, but these do not affect the overall group.

Recently the 80586 microchip has been launched, but at the time of writing there are no commercially available machines in the market that use this chip and we won't consider them any further in this book. So much for the history of the PC.

The main purpose of this book is to tell you how the storage devices, i.e. the hard disk drives function, how to install them in your system, fault finding and (hopefully) curing, preventative maintenance, testing and understanding the way the data is organised.

Data Storage

The history of data storage is as old as Mankind itself. The earliest known examples of data storage are the spectacular paintings to be found in the caves at Lascaux, France. These pictures date from the Palaeolithic period which commenced around 2.5 to 3 million years ago. The actual date of the paintings cannot be accurately assessed but there is no doubt that they are the creation of Mankind's early ancestors.

From that early beginning we have moved on to pitted marks in clay, to characters on Papyrus, stone, slate, paper and thence to recording information in or on devices that require special machines to decipher it, and finally to storing information on computers.

Electronic storage of data began with Thomas Edison but this did not involve electronics! Amongst many dozens of inventions, Mr Edison gave us the gramophone. Into one end went raw sound waves which were recorded on to a cylinder of wax. As soon as the sound had stopped, the recording was available to be listened to. The original gramophone did not use electricity, it worked by means of a clockwork motor to drive the cylinder and simple air pressure did the rest. Mr Edison fiddled about a lot with magnetism and it has always surprised me that he did not invent the forerunner of modern magnetic data storage, the Wire Recorder.

The wire recorder has two spools of incredibly thin wire, (a spool could contain several miles of the stuff), which is pulled off one spool, past an assembly containing a small electromagnet and then collected on the other spool. A small amplifier raises the output of a microphone and feeds the electromagnet which varies the magnetism according to the sound that is fed in. This gives rise to varying amounts of induced magnetism in the bit of wire that is passing the head at any particular time.

To reproduce the same sound, the wire has to be wound back to the starting point and pulled past the electromagnet. This time the input and output of the amplifier are reversed. The head is now connected to the input and the output is connected to a loudspeaker. As the magnetised wire is drawn past the head, the varying amount of magnetism affects the head and induces an electric current which is amplified and then comes out of the speaker.

Wire recorders suffered from many problems, not least of which was the ability of the wire to detect the most important point of whatever was being recorded and choose that moment to break! The wire, being made of a steel alloy, was extremely difficult to repair. Other problems were associated with very poor signal to noise ratio, and the sheer size and weight of the recorder.

In the late 1930's and early 1940's the Germans spent a lot of time pushing the wire recorder to its limits, which was not far. Then some bright spark had the idea of coating a paper tape with a powder containing a mixture of iron oxides which would hold a magnetic 'charge'. This worked and over the next few years was developed to a very high degree. Thus the Tape Recorder was born.

The original paper rapidly disappeared, to be replaced with a tape using a plastic base, these days it is usually polyester or mylar. The surface coating is no longer any old iron oxide that just happens to be lying around, instead there are many different compounds used and the various manufacturers guard their formulae very carefully.

The tape is supplied on plastic or metal spools and is made in a wide range of sizes, 1/8, 1/4, 1/2, 1 and 2 inches being the most commonly available. The principle is the same as the wire recorder; the tape is drawn past a Recording/Replay head at a constant speed. The speed depends on the quality of the machine and what is being recorded. The speed in a cassette recorder is usually 1.75-inch per second while a 48 track machine, as found in a recording studio and using 2-inch wide tape, will run at 30-inch per second.

The next development came in the early 1960's with the introduction of the tape cassette. Created and patented by Philips Electronics in Holland, the cassette recorder very quickly became a standard, almost wiping the reel to reel tape recorders off the face of the earth, except for 'serious' amateurs and for professional purposes. The reason for the popularity of the cassette recorder's meteoric rise was simple - the tape packaging. No longer did you have to fiddle about threading the tape through a series of rollers, past heads and onto another reel. The cassette contains two hubs to which the tape is firmly attached. The tape runs from one hub to the other over a series of rollers and there is a spring loaded felt pad for the record/replay head to press the tape against for good contact. The drive spindle and pinch-wheel all gain access through the cutouts in the cassette casing. All the user has to do is put the cassette in the correct way round and it works! A very simple and effective way to record sound or data.

For data storage purposes, tape suffers from one inherent design fault. The medium, i.e. the tape, is linear. This means that the recorded information is stored along the length, and because it has closed ends, it is impossible to get easy random access to the information. Such a method is called serial storage. In fact, because of the design of the domestic cassette recorder usually used with micro computers, it is impossible to get random access at all!

There are two ways to achieve pseudo-random access on a tape based storage system. The first is to use a cassette that does not have closed ends on the tape, in other words the tape must be in the form of an endless loop, and the second is to use very high speed. A good example of the first type can be found in some telephone answering machines. The message that the caller hears is on a cassette that contains a loop of tape with a metallic ribbon placed somewhere along its length, usually across the join. The recorder has a sensor that can detect the start/finish of the tape. The electronics can then use this to start and stop both the outgoing message and the incoming message recorder. The problem with serial storage is that you usually need a lot of tape and a loop is prone to tangle.

The second type, which is actually much slower than true random access tape storage, is the one usually portrayed on television - the rows of cabinets with two wheels shuffling backwards and forwards. Those are high speed tape drives, shunting backwards and forwards at a high rate of knots, reading and writing data. The tape is usually 1/2-inch wide and tape drives are available that can handle up to 4,800 feet of tape on one spool. There are usually 7 data tracks and the information is recorded at the rate of 7,500 bits per inch. Neither of these types of tape storage can be used as true random storage. However, because of the speeds involved in shuttling the tape backwards and forwards, this type of storage can appear to be random access. True random access to the data available requires a completely different storage medium.

The solution was to use large drums of metal coated with a magnetic material on its outer surface - the original cylinders. The surface of the drum was divided up into a series of parallel tracks, each of which was further sub-divided into sectors. These drums rotated at approximately 3,000 RPM but their access times were not very fast, typically about 50 milliseconds although this speed could be increased by using a large number of Read/Write Heads. Ultimately, drum storage was unwieldy and even large cylinders had storage capacities of less than 10 Mb. In addition to this the drums required specialised storage conditions and were consigned to providing backup storage before they finally vanished. They left their legacy with some of the terminology used. Because of the way the Read/Write Heads were arranged, each head could be considered separately from the others, in fact the whole drum could be considered to be a series of 'cylinders' all joined together. The term 'cylinder' lingers on to this day.

A tidier solution came with the advent of disk storage. This consisted of a number, usually 6, of large discs, mounted one above the other on a central spindle. The discs were coated with magnetic material on each side and the Read/ Write Heads moved between the platters to access the information. The individual disc could hold roughly 500 Kb of data - although the capacity varied enormously from manufacturer to manufacturer. These hard discs were to become the primary storage medium of most mainframe computers and are still used to this day.

However in computer terms the tape cassette still refuses to die. Unlike the hard disk which is spinning all the time the machine is switched on, the tape is only running when it is actually needed. This reduction in 'run time' means that the tape drive is apparently more reliable and tape drives of many different types are still widely used in the industry, but almost exclusively as a means of data backup. The complete contents of a hard disk are run on to a tape cassette at (supposedly) regular intervals and provide a snapshot of what is on the system's disk drive at the time the backup is done. The tape backup units come in several different formats and are normally very reliable.

Chapter 2
Floppy Disks

Overview

Floppy disks have been the backbone of the computer industry for so long that everyone takes them for granted. In actuality hard disks, at least on mainframes, preceded floppies by a considerable number of years. Here we are going to concentrate on floppy disks as used in any PC, XT or AT and we will cover all the various types and standards in detail.

Before we start let's get one thing crystal clear. Disks are spelled with a K - never with a C. The reason is quite simple. The word disk is a contraction of diskette. Even if you check the spelling in the Oxford English Dictionary or any other good dictionary you will find that they refer to computer storage media as disk.

Diskette was the word originally applied to the portable, non-rigid, magnetic storage medium used by mainframe computers. At the time, their standard storage media were huge, usually 14-inch diameter fixed disks, arranged in stacks of six that had to be specially protected. They also used great reels of magnetic tape that need to be handled very carefully. The trouble with using either of these is that they tend to be heavy, you can't go around with a stack or even a reel under your arm. Put simply, they lack portability.

What was needed was something light and readily transportable. It didn't need to have very high capacity but it did have to be large enough to contain the important information. The result was flexible discs of plastic, coated with a magnetisable material and encased in a semi-rigid sleeve. Because the elements of the hard disks were called discs someone coined the new term diskettes, i.e. baby discs, for the new creation. Because people are inherently lazy, the word was soon shortened to disks and it has remained so ever since. Only purists add the 'ette' to the end of the word!

With the advent of the Personal Computer in 1981, IBM quickly found that they needed a better storage medium than the cassette tapes that the original used. They decided to use smaller disks, after all they had been involved with main frames for a good many years and so were familiar with the capabilities of the disks. They decided to use a 5.25-inch disk and this became the de facto standard for all PC's thereafter.

The original disk could store only 160 Kb of data but this was later upgraded to 180 Kb and then to 360 Kb. Today you can get high capacity disks that will store 2.8 Mb, or nearly 20 times the amount you could store on one of the originals. (There was also a 720 Kb 5.25-inch disk but it was rarely used commercially and so it quickly vanished.) Sony are believed to be working on a floppy disk with a capacity of 20 Megabytes! In reality, 5.25-inch disks are not as durable or as well protected as many people would like to think. It is very easy to damage the coating, by putting your fingers onto the exposed surface for instance. In addition only a small portion of the entire disk is used to record information, so much so that nearly 3/4 of the disk is unused.

Today, many machines are fitted with the smaller and more compact 3.5-inch disks. These are much more durable, better protected and have twice the storage capacity of their early 5.25-inch cousins. These new disks come in two sizes, 720 Kb and 1.44 Mb. But nothing stands still, especially in the computer industry. The Japanese have perfected a 2-inch disk that can store over 2 Mb, but unfortunately it is only fitted to certain Japanese machines that are hardly ever exported. There are now commercial examples of a 3.5-inch disk with a capacity of 20 Mb and although rare, we expect to see them fitted to machines in the latter half of 1992. You can be sure that the floppy storage will continue to get smaller, while increasing its capacity. For all that though, the 5.25-inch disk will be around for some time to come; there are just too many of them in circulation for them to vanish overnight.

Construction

All floppy disks, regardless of their size, are made of a non-woven polyester, the most important property of which is that it is virtually impossible to tear and it has a massive amount of resistance to lateral movement. You can tear a floppy disk, but only if it has been nicked or otherwise cut first or you are very very strong. It also has the advantage of having a very low co-efficient of expansion so low that in can safely be ignored.

To make disks, the manufacturers take huge, 10 feet wide rolls of plastic and coat both sides of it with an epoxy resin containing magnetic material. In the case of low capacity disks this is normally ultra-fine ferrous material; for high capacity disks they use a cobalt based preparation. The plastic is then rolled again to spread the coating to an even thickness and polish the surface. The resultant rolls are placed in large ovens where they are heat treated for a number of days until the resin has dried evenly. Thereafter the rolls are removed and cut into large sheets from which the correct sized discs are punched out. They are called cookies at this stage and they are essentially finished. Finally the cookies are encased in their sleeves, inside a protected inner liner, of semi-rigid PVC for 5.25-inch disks or rigid PVC for 3.5-inch ones. 3.5-inch disks also have a metal hub affixed to them and the sleeve has a thin, spring loaded metal protector at the business end.

If you look closely at a floppy disk you will notice the construction details. While the two sizes have several things in common they also have a number of unique properties so we'll examine them in turn. Take the 5.25-inch one first; it does not matter whether it is 360 Kb or 1.2 Mb as they have the same basic design. Place it so that it is face up. The most prominent feature is the large hole in the middle. This is the Central Hub Access Hole, to give it its proper name, and it may or may not have a strengthening ring in it. When you place the disk into a drive, a central spindle or HUB moves up and aligns itself with this hole so that the disk will be properly aligned to be read from or written to.

To one side of the large hole is a smaller hole called the Index Hole.There is actually a hole in the disk itself that will align with this. If you turn the disk carefully, from the centre, you will eventually come to it. The Index Hole is used by the computer, actually by the operating system via the drive, to mark the beginning of the sectors on the disk. (We'll cover sectors later.) There should be only one hole in the disk itself which tells you that the disk is soft-sectored. This means that the operating system can put as many sectors as it wishes onto the disk. If you find that your disk has more than one hole then it is hard sectored and the best thing you can do with it is use it as a coaster - hard sectored disks should not be used in any personal computer.

Immediately below the Central Hub Access Hole is a lozenge shaped opening that exposes the actual disk surface. This is the Media Access Point. This is where the Read/Write Heads make contact with the disk so that the computer can use it. (In actuality the heads don't make contact with the disk, or they shouldn't, but are separated from it by about 10 microns.) Below the Media

Access Point and on either side of it, are two semi-circular notches. These are the Stress Relief Notches and their purpose is to prevent the disk being flexed too far. If you try to bend the disk laterally, do it gently, you will find that the disk sleeve flexes around these points. It they were not there then the disk itself would bend and become unusable.

Finally, on the right hand side of the disk, about an inch from the top, you will see that a rectangular piece has been punched out of the sleeve. This is the Write Enable Hole. If this is missing or covered over then you cannot write to that disk.

A 3.5-inch disk is rather different - you cannot see the actual disk at all, unless you open the gate. For 720 Kb disks the case is usually blue, high capacity disks are normally black. The rigid plastic case serves two functions. Firstly, it offers much better protection against accidental damage than the sleeve on its larger cousin does. Secondly, it helps to stabilise the disk in the drive and that is one reason why they can be used to store more information.

The most noticeable feature of these disks is the metal shutter at the bottom of the case. This moves sideways when you place the disk into the drive and exposes the surface to the heads. You can move this yourself and see the disk inside the case.

Turn the disk over and look at the back. Instead of a large hole, the 3.5-inch disk has a complex metal hub which is actually bonded to the disk inside. This is necessary to make sure that the disk aligns correctly in the drive.

At the top of the disk, on the left hand side, is a small piece of black plastic lying in a channel covering a square hole. This is the Write Protect feature. When the tab is up, i.e. the hole is exposed, then the disk is Write Protected. If the hole is covered then you can write to the disk. (Some 3.5-inch disk labels have a reminder printed on them about this.) You can make a disk permanently Write Protected by removing the slider, but be careful how you remove it.

Finally, and on high capacity disks only, there is a round hole on the right hand side. This is the Media Density Selector Hole. If the hole is present then the disk is high capacity and can be formatted to 1.44 Mb - otherwise it cannot.

While 3.5-inch disks are more durable than the larger ones, e.g. you can drop them onto a desk, they are still rather fragile. Don't use them as coasters or Frisbees and don't put them on a radiator. If you do then you are likely to lose the data they contain.

Types and Specifications

Disks come in a bewildering range of types and bear all kinds of strange and confusing labels. Here is a brief run-down of what the terms mean.

Soft Sectored disks have a single hole in the disk itself that marks the position of the first sector. You should only use soft sectored disks.

Hard Sectored disks have a number of holes in the disk. It is pointless to use hard sectored disks in a personal computer because the operating system will not know what to do with them.

Single Sided disks are now rather rare. In reality there was never any such thing as the cookies are always coated on both sides. It was the drives that made a difference, not the disks.

Double Sided disks are the norm. The difference between these and previous type is that they are certified, i.e. checked, on both sides. Single sided disks are checked only on the facing side. You can generally use either single or double sided disks with safety, except in a high capacity drive where the quality of the disk coating is different. If you get a large number of bad sectors on a disk then don't use it - throw it away. (In reality all floppy disks are coated on both sides - if not they would buckle.)

Double Density is the standard for all of the lower capacity disks, either 5.25 or 3.5-inch. In the case of the former they are designed to allow 48 tracks per inch and a storage rate of 5,876 bits per inch of track length. Thus they have a total capacity of 360 Kb.

In the case of 3.5-inch disks they will allow 135 tpi and a track capacity of 8,717 bits per inch. Their total capacity is therefore 720 Kb.

Quad Density only applied to 5.25-inch disks. These could be formatted to 96 tracks per inch but they retain the original packing rate. Thus they would allow 720 Kb per disk. However these disks were never really used in any quantity as they were superseded by High Density drives and disks.

High Density disks are coated with a cobalt based preparation which can be magnetised with a weaker field strength - not a higher one as you might expect. It has to be weaker because the tracks and bytes per inch capacity are higher. If the field strength was also higher there would be an increased risk of cross contamination on the disk surface.

5.25-inch High Capacity disks have 96 tracks per inch which will allow 9,646 bits per inch to be packed into them. Their formatted capacity is 1.20 Mb or 1,228.8 Kb.

3.5-inch High Capacity disks have 135 tpi, the same as the lower density ones, but they will allow a packing rate of nearly 17,434 bits per inch of track length. Thus their total formatted capacity is 1.44 Mb.

Truth and Fallacy

This section is intended to dispel some of the common fears and incorrect information that people have about floppy disks.

You can format double density disks as high density.

True-ish. You can format a standard disk as high capacity but you will get an awful lot of bad sectors, i.e. areas that the operating system cannot write to. In addition, you are making the drive work harder than it needs to and you also risk losing any data you put onto such a disk. The magnetic coating on DD and High Capacity disks is different; the former is based on ferrous material while the latter uses a cobalt compound. This is because the HC drive uses a weaker magnetic field and so the material on the disk has to be of a higher quality. When you format a standard disk in a standard drive the tracks are approximately 0.36 mm wide. On a HC drive they are only 0.11 mm wide and the sides of them have to be 'trimmed' to make them fit properly and prevent them leaking into each other. When you format the standard disk in the HC drive the tracks are laid down as the 0.11 mm width but the material is not capable of maintaining these. Gradually, over a period of time, the magnetic fluxes deteriorate and so the data is lost. In addition, the disk is then useless as a standard capacity disk because that drive finds one set of tracks apparently embedded in another and so it will return an 'unusable media' error message.

Airport X-ray machines can damage disks, it is a wise precaution to ask for them to be hand examined rather than allow them to go through an X-ray machine.

In a word - balderdash. Disks can only be damaged by magnetic fields, either real or induced, and the airport security X-Ray device does not use any. In fact this is the safest place to put your disks because it is shielded against magnetism. The worst thing you can do is carry them through the gateway, which is actually a giant metal detector. This does use magnetism and so your disks stand a very good chance of being corrupted.

Heat will damage the disk.

True. Any floppy disk, or hard disk for that matter, is very susceptible to changes in temperature. If you look on some disk sleeves, the paper ones, you will find that they carry a temperature tolerance range, usually 10 to 50 degrees Centigrade. This is the temperature at which the disk can be assumed to work correctly. However don't try heating it from the lower value to the higher in a single step by placing it on a radiator for example - or you will suddenly find it does not work. A stable temperature is best, but failing that, one that fluctuates very slowly will do. In addition, the relative humidity of the environment will affect the disk.

Sunlight damages disks.

True-ish. It is not the light that harms them but rather the increase in temperature that will accompany this. See previous page. Don't forget that sunlight beaming through a window can reach very high temperatures and easily heat a disk lying in it, which after all is black and therefore radiation absorbing, very quickly.

Floppy disks gradually lose their magnetic field.

Essentially not true. Providing that you take care to store the disk in an environment that lies within the tolerance range then the disk will have a life expectancy of 20-30 years.

Static electricity damages the disk.

Again this is true-ish. What causes the damage is the massive burst of electricity that occurs when you, or another device loaded with static, touch the disk. At the point, which will normally be no larger than a pin prick, where the discharge touches the disk the temperature can be as much as 200 degrees Celsius. This will definitely mess up the magnetic flux at that point and at the points around it. The damage, and its severity, will radiate from that point like ripples on a pond.

Touching the actual disk will ruin it.

This is not as true as it sounds - although it can be taken as true. What actually happens is that you place a layer of oil and dirt onto the disk, regardless of how clean your hands are. This is then transferred to the Read/Write Heads when you put the disk into the drive and read it. This oil and dirt then attracts more of the same until, eventually, the heads become excessively worn or damaged. You should clean your disk drive heads, using any of the proprietary cleaners, at least once a quarter - more if your machine is heavily used. But don't overdo it because that is just as bad.

Keeping the disk in a storage box beside the computer is a good idea.

No it is not! The majority of monitors have a degaussing coil in them, the sole purpose of which is to demagnetise the elements of the monitor every time you turn it on. This is done using a high intensity magnetic field - televisions do the same thing by the way - and it extends for about 18" all round the front of the monitor. Therefore if you place a disk near this it stands a good chance of being damaged. Telephones and loudspeakers also use a magnetic field by the way.

Writing on the label with a pen damages the disk.

Not necessarily. It depends on how much force you use when writing. The sleeve of even a standard floppy disk is quite resilient and the inner liner helps to dissipate any localised force. However, to be on the safe side, write the labels before sticking them on or else use a felt tipped pen.

Floppy Disk Drives

Having the floppy disks is all well and good but you must have the correct type of drive for the particular disk - don't use DD disks in a High Capacity drive or vice versa. Once a disk is placed in the drive and the door is shut, the Spindle moves upwards, grasps the disk and aligns it properly.

When you read from or write to the disk, the drive begins to spin it at either 300 RPM if it is a standard drive or 360 RPM if it is high capacity. Once it has reached optimum speed the Read/ Write Heads can then move on either side of the disk and so access the data on it. The heads move over the 1-inch wide band where the data is, or will be, recorded.

Every floppy disk drive contains the same basic components. At the front, i.e. the bit that you normally see, is the faceplate or Bezel. This contains the door latch, an LED indicator and a slot into which the disk is placed. The bezel is removable and is generally only needed for cosmetic purposes although it does help to stabilise the unit within the carrier.

At the back of the drive unit are two terminals. The first is the power connector. It has four little pins, into which is plugged a lead from the computer's power supply. The second, a 34-pin connector, is connected by a ribbon cable to the drive controller and it is through this that the data and control signals are transmitted.

The IBM PS2 range is slightly different, the power and data cable are combined to form one 40 way ribbon cable, however this does exactly the same job as the normal drive's two cables.

Within the drive unit itself, the most important part is the Read/Write Head assembly. This consists of two heads, one on each arm, that are connected together so that they move as a single unit. (These days single head units are as rare as Dodo feathers.) The heads are made of a hard ferrous compound and contain the electromagnetic coils that do the work of reading and writing to the disk. Each of the heads is actually dual purpose, the main part of it is the recording head while at either side of this lie the erase heads.

The heads use a technique known as Tunnel Erasure to record information on the disk. As the track is laid down, or as information is placed on the track, the erase heads trim the edges of it so that it has a crisp clean edge. In this way the likelihood of one track impinging on another is minimised.

The Read/Write Heads assembly is spring loaded and it actually grips the disk itself with a light pressure, which is why disks gradually become unusable as the magnetic media is gradually worn away. This is another reason for cleaning the heads regularly.

The head assembly is moved by the Head Actuator Motor. This moves the head unit at a tangent across the surface of the disk, always in the same straight line. All floppy disk drives use what is known as a Stepper to move the heads. Such a device cannot rotate completely, it can only turn so far in one direction and then back again. The amount it can move is fixed, and the increment is called a detent, although a single movement does not have to be the entire distance it can rotate. When you ask to read information from the disk, the operating system tells the motor to move to a particular detent position because that is where the track is located, and thus it can locate the data. Each detent corresponds to a single track. Therefore a standard 5.25-inch drive motor has 40 detents, while a HC drive will have 80, ss do 3.5-inch drives which have the same number. The circular motion of the stepper is converted into a linear motion either by way of a steel band fastened to the head assembly (the most common with 5.25" drives), or by a coarse screw thread.

The stepper motor has a complete travel time of approximately 200 milliseconds. To find the average access time you take this amount and divide it by two, and then by three. Add both answers together and then divide them by two. This gives a result of 83 milliseconds which is roughly the time it will take the heads to move from one track to another random track.

The disk is spun by the Spindle Motor. All modern drives use direct drive motors. These are quicker and cheaper to make and have the added advantage that there is no need to manually adjust the rotational speed, this is done electronically. The Spindle itself is simply a cylindrical piece of metal that possesses a shaped head which fits into the Central Hub Hole of the disk and holds it steady in the drive.

All disk drives contain circuit boards, generally called Logic Boards, which contain all the necessary circuitry to control the electromechanical parts of the drive unit as well as the interface to the controller. This interface is standard to all drives and is the Shugart Associates SA-450. This was originally created by Allen Shugart in the Seventies, before he left to found Seagate Technology, and it is used in the vast majority of personal computer disk drives. The advantage of using such a standard is that you can take any disk drive, put it into a computer and be sure that it will work. (Although you also have to bear in mind the problems of the operating system using particular sizes of drive.)

In order to use the drive you must also have a controller card that fits into one of the computer's expansion slots. There are two commonly used controller chips, one from Western Digital - the 8272, and the other from NEC - the UPD765. The chips are effectively interchangeable because they use the same standard.

The chips are contained on a plug-in card assembly. Some OEM's use a different card that also contains the serial port, but generally speaking these only appear on older machines.

Fitting a Second Drive

As all computers come with at least one floppy drive it is not worth covering fitting one, but many people will want to install a second drive. This is how to do it.

Both of the standard controller cards are capable of interfacing with two drives, so you do not normally need to purchase a second one. However you may have to get a new cable. Some computers come with a ribbon cable that has only one connector on it, which joins onto the back of the original floppy drive. However many machines come with a ribbon that has two female connectors and only one of them is used for the in situ drive. The second one will connect the new unit.

If you get a new drive be sure you get the right one. The units for an XT and an AT are different. This is because all AT's use pin 34 to carry a Disk Change-line Signal - XT's don't use this pin at all because they cannot use the signal. The change-line signal is used to tell the AT that the disk has been changed. The reason it needs to know this is because the operating system only reads the root directory entry the first time it encounters the disk, thereafter it holds the information in its memory. Only when the disk is changed will it read the root directory again. This makes the disk operation much faster and so speeds up the access time.

If you use the wrong drive, it may send the wrong signal and this will confuse the operating system so that it does not read the next disk but retains the directory of the first one. No matter what you do, you cannot get rid of it except by a complete reboot and even that will not work all the time. Just to confuse matters further, there are virtually no drives made purely for one machine or the other!

When ordering the drive, specify that you need it for an XT or for an AT, the supplier will merely change a couple of 'links' on the drive to make it suitable for your system. In fact many modern drives don't even need to have links changed, they are capable of working on either type of computer without modification.

To install the drive, turn off the power and open the computer case - usually by removing a number of screws on the back and sliding the top cover off. The drives are housed in the Carrier Unit. On some computers this entire thing can be removed, while on others it cannot. Personally, we find it easier not to bother taking it out - it is a bit fiddly leaving it in place but taking it out and replacing it is too much hassle. Undo the screws that hold the cover plate of the empty slot where you want the drive to go; normally this will be directly under the existing drive unit because the ribbon cables are not very long. Slide the cover out, being careful not to bash the other drives in the process.

Unpack the new unit. DO NOT touch any of the exposed pins on the logic board. They are extremely sensitive to electric and magnetic currents, even the minute amounts that exist in the human body. Check the drive manual so you can set the Drive Select Jumpers correctly. These are switches that tell the controller which drive is which and they must be set correctly. Unfortunately there is no set standard for this, unless you have a pure IBM machine and are using drives purchased from IBM, so it is best to consult the manual. The manual for your system will tell you about the Terminating Resistor, which stops any backlash signal from reaching the controller, and this must be placed correctly on the drive that will be A:, i.e. the lowest lettered drive.

Once you have done that you simply slide the drive unit into the carrier and lay it gently onto the bottom of the carrier or the top of an existing drive. Connect the power cable and the connecting block and then boot up the machine - before you secure the drive into the carrier.

Try out the new drive - put a disk into it and read something from it, write it back and format a blank disk. If everything works okay then turn off the power again and fix the drive unit to the carrier using the screws. Replace the computer case cover, replace its screws and then reboot again. That's all there is to it. On some computers you will also have to run a special program called, usually, SETUP before you can use the drive. The program identifies the drive to the operating system, and then stores the information in the non-volatile RAM, so the computer knows about the drive's existence. Make sure you identify the drive correctly (remember it can be one of four types) or it will not work.

If the drive does not work, e.g. it won't write to the new disk, then check all the connections and settings you have made. If you are absolutely certain that they conform to the OEM manual instructions and it still does not work, then the drive is probably damaged. This only happens on very rare occasions but if you are unlucky then get back to the dealer from whom you purchased the drive as soon as possible, and they should replace it for you.

Disk Drive Operation

At its simplest, you put a disk into the drive, the disk then spins at the correct speed, the Read/Write Heads move across it reading or writing data. However, this is only a thin surface gloss over what actually happens; the reality is a little more complex.

All floppy disks, as previously mentioned, are coated with a magnetisable material. A good analogy for a new disk is a completely blank sheet of paper. In order to write on it neatly and precisely you must first draw lines on it. This is what the FORMAT command does. It takes the blank disk and organises the coating into Tracks and Sectors and it also creates the Boot, FAT and Root directories entries on the disk so that the operating system can use it.

The tracks are a series of concentric circles, not a spiral, laid out on the disk. Depending on which capacity you are using there will be a different number of tracks and they will be of different widths.

A 360 Kb disk has 40 Tracks and they are 0.33 mm wide.

1.2 Mb disks have 80 Tracks and they are 0.16 mm wide.

Both types of 3.5-inch disk have 80 Tracks and they are 0.115 mm wide. It is the number of sectors (see below) which changes the capacity.

If you record information on a disk in a 360 Kb drive and then read it and try to rewrite it in a 1.2 Mb drive you may run into problems. The reason is because of the different track widths. As far as the computer is concerned one track is embedded in another and therefore the entire disk is useless. You can only recover such a disk by using a bulk eraser which degausses the entire disk. In addition to the track width, the strength of the magnetism used on each disk varies according to type. HC drives use a magnetic field that is only half the strength of standard capacity drives.

However this problem is gradually disappearing. Modern high capacity drives do not usually have a problem reading, writing and formatting either capacity of disk.

Once the tracks are laid down the operating system then divides them into Sectors. The number of sectors depends on the capacity.

> 5.25-inch 360 Kb and 3.5-inch 720 Kb disks have 9 sectors per track.
>
> 5.25-inch 1.2 Mb disks have 15 sectors.
>
> 3.5-inch 1.44 Mb disks have 18 sectors.

Because each sector, regardless of the number per track, holds 512 bytes of information you can then work out the total storage capacity of a disk as in the table below. (Don't forget that there are two sides.)

Size	Tracks	Sectors	Capacity
5.25-inch	40	9	360 Kb
5.25-inch	80	15	1,200 Kb
3.5-inch	80	9	720 Kb
3.5-inch	80	18	1,440 Kb

However, when it comes to allocating storage space on the disks, MS-DOS makes use of things called Clusters. These are simply a multiple of sectors and a cluster is the minimum amount of space that any file can fit into. On both the lower capacity disks the cluster size is 2 sectors, or 1,024 bytes, while on HC disks it is only a single sector. The reason HC disks use smaller cluster sizes is simply because the disks are faster. Because the cluster size is the minimum amount of space a file can occupy, you will get some odd-seeming readings when you use the DIR command.

For example, a file that is 32 Bytes will occupy 1 Kb of a double density disk or 512 Bytes on a HC disk. It is when you have files that are 1,025 Bytes that the problem becomes acute. Such a file will occupy 2 Kb of a DD disk but only 1.5 Kb on a HC disk.

On any disk, the operating system will automatically retain a certain amount of the capacity for its own use, e.g. 6 Kb on a 360 Kb disk and 11.5 Kb on a 1.2 Mb one, and thus the usable capacity is always less than the total. This space used to store the Boot, Fat and Root.

The Boot Sector is always stored at Track 0, Sector 1. (The tracks are numbered 0 to 79, while the sectors are numbered starting with 1.) It contains all the information about the number of Tracks, Sectors per Track and Bytes per Sector, along with other identifying information that the operating system needs in order to be able to use the disk.

Following on from the Boot Sector is the File Allocation Table, FAT for short. This is literally a table of entries that keeps track of what sectors are allocated to which file, where they start and continue and what sectors are currently free and ready for use. When you delete a file what actually happens is that the filename, as recorded in the FAT, is changed so that its initial letter becomes the Greek character Sigma. This tells the operating system that the sectors previously allocated to that file can now be overwritten with new information. This is why you can recover 'deleted' files. The utility program looks for all the files that begin with Sigma and then gives you a chance to rename them and so recover them. However, if you have written something else to the disk since the erasure then the sectors are likely to already have been reused and so the file may be lost for good.

The final part of the reserved space is the Root Directory. This contains detailed information about the files on the disk, their size, time and date stamping, along with the Volume Label of the disk if any.

Whenever you write to a disk, the operating system will always try to use the first available space on the disk. On a newly formatted disk this does not matter but on a well used disk it can slow down the access time. Consider a disk that is used constantly; it has data written to it, read from it and deleted off it. The remaining files will be scattered all over the available sectors but there will be 'holes' where sectors have been freed When you next write to the disk, MS-DOS stores as much of the file as possible in the first available space. If the file won't all fit at that location then MS-DOS stores the next chunk in the nearest 'hole' and so on until the entire file has been written to the disk. The result is that the file can be stored in different sectors all over the disk Such a file is said to be non-contiguous and it slows down the access time.

The problem is not too great on a standard floppy disk; after all MS-DOS was designed to handle disk files in just this way. However, when you come to use high capacity or hard disks then it can be a real problem. Fortunately, there are a range of utility programs available that can solve the problem and make all the files contiguous, as you will see later.

Chapter 3
Hard Disks

Construction

A hard disk is an enclosed box, which contains the mechanical parts of the drives, and a backing plate which contains the electronics. The entire thing is a single unit and it fits into the mounting bay, normally at the front of the computer, and is secured by four small screws. At the back of the drive are the connectors, two thin blocks to which are connected ribbon cables that enable the drive to communicate with the controller, and the power input, four vertical pins to which the power supply is fixed. Within the box are the platters, spindle, motor and Read/Write heads. An important point to realise about all disk drives, particularly hard disks, is that you must apply the RTM principle - i.e. Read The Manual.

While all hard disk drives are essentially the same there are a huge range of drive units available and it is important that you know which you are using. For example the Controller, see later, makes an enormous difference. An RLL drive and a MFM drive are mutually incompatible - placing two different controllers in the one machine can lead to drastic problems.

The name 'Hard Disk Drive' exists because that is it exactly what it is - the disks within the device, called 'Platters', are made of aluminium which is then coated with a magnetic material. Thus the disks are hard, hence the name.

Another nomenclature is Fixed Disk - this is because the platters themselves are not removable. If you want to take out any of the platters you need to remove the entire disk assembly.

Finally there is a third name applied to the device, that of Winchester Disks . No-one is exactly sure of how the name came about but there are two generally accepted derivations:

1) One legend is that originally the hard disk drive was developed at a plant in Winchester, Mass. The name of the town was then applied to the devices.

2) The second possible story is that IBM created a hard disk drive in the 1960's which had 30 Mb of fixed disk storage but it also had 30 Mb of removable storage. The drives were called 30-30. Americans being notable gun enthusiasts, a very popular rifle made by the Winchester company was also called the same name, hence the connection.

Over the years the name for any hard disk became Winchester and you can believe which ever version of the story you wish. All three names; Hard Disk, Fixed Disk or Winchester Disk, are totally interchangeable. They all mean exactly the same thing - a series of platters, stacked one above the other and enclosed in an airtight box.

The hard disk drive has two distinct parts; the HDA, the Hard Disk Assembly, and the electronics. The number of platters in the HDA will depend on the size and capacity of the drive. The size is also known as the 'Form Factor'. In drives designed for use in a personal computer there are only two normal form factors, 5.25-inch or 3.5-inch. The size refers to the diameter of the disks. In addition to the platters the HDA also includes the Read/ Write Heads and the other mechanical bits and pieces. The electronics are usually mounted beneath the HDA on a backplate. This also contains the connectors, that are joined to the Controller Board by ribbon cables, and the four-pin power input point.

The complete unit, i.e. the disk assembly and control circuitry are normally the same size as a 5.25-inch floppy disk drive, which after all is the original standard for disk drive sizes, and this allows them to be fitted easily into the normal mounting bay at the front of the machine. Most disk drive manufacturers supply 3.5-inch drives mounted on a frame of the same size, even though the platters themselves are smaller and the entire drive is more compact. However some machines have a drive mounting bay hidden away inside the system box which will only allow the fitting of a 3.5-inch half-height drive.

As we have already said, the platters are made of an aluminium alloy, the thickness depends on the manufacturer of the drive. We have seen platters that were 4 millimetres thick, which is exceptional, while the thinnest we have ever seen are a mere 1 millimetre, again this is exceptional. Normally platters will fall midway between these two. NEC are now using a platter with a thickness of 1.5 millimetres as standard in all the 3.5" drives they make.

The platter is stamped out of a sheet of aluminium, the edges are then polished and the surface is checked for flaws. Even a tiny imperfection of less than 50 millionths of an inch will make the platter unusable! A coating is then applied to the raw platters and this is the part that will be magnetised to hold the data at the end of the day. There are two types of coating media, a ferrous oxide or an arcane film. Every manufacturer uses a different coating, rather like MacDonalds and Burger King using different recipes for their burgers, and their 'recipe' is a closely guarded secret. The result is that you can never know exactly what the coating contains - but as long as it works does it matter? In reality there is very little difference between the various coatings - not that the manufacturers would agree.

With lower capacity drives the surface coating is applied as a mixture containing the ferrous material in a resin carrier. Once the coating has been applied, the disk is spun at high speed which centrifugally spreads the coating to a uniform thickness. The platters are then cured in a rigidly temperature-controlled oven. Once they have cooled, both surfaces are polished to a very high degree of accuracy of both smoothness and surface flatness. An oxide coating is usually about 32 millionths of an inch thick.

High capacity drives use 'Plated Media'. This is another name for 'Thin Film Media', so called because the coating is extremely thin, it can be as little as 2 millionths of an inch. The platter is made in the same way as above but the surface is much more carefully polished and checked before the coating is applied. This is done by electrolysis. The platters are immersed in a series of baths containing different solutions that coat the substrate with layers of metallic film. The last coating is usually a cobalt alloy about 1 millionth of an inch thick.

An alternative method is called Sputtered Coating. This provides the most perfect and thinnest surface that can currently be produced. The disks are prepared in the same way as for plated media and they are then coated with a layer of nickel phosphorus. The nickel coating is the one that provides a surface of uniform flatness and a mirror like finish. A surface coating of a cobalt alloy is then applied in a vacuum by a process known as sputtering. The cobalt is then covered in a very thin layer of a hard carbon compound.

If you were to open a hard disk drive and look at the platters (but we recommend that you don't actually do so), what you would see would depend very much on the capacity and manufacturer of that particular unit. In general a 20 Mb drive will have brown or amber coloured disks. The higher capacity drives will have a silver or black mirror-like surface.

The number of platters within the drive unit will depend on the capacity of the drive, 20 Mb drives usually have 2 platters, i.e. four sides, while high capacity drives can have up to 8 platters.

Spindle Motors

Inside the HDA, the platters are all mounted on the shaft. This is called the Spindle and it operates much the same as a floppy drive spindle except that it does not move up and down. The platters and the spindle are fixed in such a way that they form a single unit. The motor that turns the platters is called, logically enough, the Spindle Motor. The rotational speed of 90% of all hard disks is 3600 revolutions per minute, although some drives rotate at 3650 RPM. Some of the larger drives being produced spin at 5400 RPM and experiments are being done with a speed of 2500 RPM.

The specification for the spindle speed on most drives allows for a speed tolerance of +/- 1%, i.e. +/- 36 RPM. To achieve that order of stability requires some very sophisticated speed measuring and controlling electronics. The operational details are outside the scope of this book, suffice it to say most drives will automatically switch themselves off if the speed goes outside the limits given above. In actuality you will find that most disk drives rotate at a speed to within 1 RPM of their design specification. For example, the Seagate ST-225 in one of our machines runs at 3600.24 RPM - an incredible degree of precision, (we used 'SpinRite' to measure the speed).

The motor is normally powered from the 12 volt supply and for the first few seconds it is switched on requires a lot of current. Typically a drive that requires 12 volts at 0.5 amp when up to speed will require 1.6 amps for the first 12 - 15 seconds of power on operation and will require 0.7 amp during Read/Write operations, i.e. whenever the heads are being moved. Some of the really big drives can require up to 8 amps during the spin to speed cycle. To help spread the load on the power supply many modern drives do not start spinning when the computer is switched on. Instead they sit and wait until they get a signal from the controller to tell them to start.

The spindle contains one of the most common causes of noise in a hard disk drive. There can be large amounts of static electricity generated because of friction. If this static charge is not allowed to discharge to ground there is a chance of it discharging through the head assembly or spindle motor bearing. If this happens the lubricants can get burned which doesn't do the bearings any good at all! On the other hand if it discharges through the heads, catastrophic damage can occur. The heads are not just bits of magnet, (see the later section on heads). So to prevent either of these effects occurring the drive has an earthing strap fitted. This is usually a strip of copper with a little carbon button bonded to it where it touches the end of the spindle. This button can wear and a little polished pit appears which can cause the whole strap to vibrate and make a really loud noise or a whining sound. This noise can be mistaken for something much more serious like a complete hard disk failure.

There are several ways of attempting a cure:

1) Remove the strap altogether. For the reasons given above this is definitely not recommended. Removing the strap will void any guarantee or warranty supplied by the manufacturer or dealer

2) Lubricate the contact point. This is usually the simplest and easiest solution. Make sure

you use a good quality Graphite lubricant. DO NOT USE ORDINARY OIL OR GREASE. Apply a single tiny drop of oil on the tip of a sharpened matchstick or a toothpick. Don't just spray it on - you must be precise.

3) Stop the strap vibrating with rubber. A small piece of rubber glued to the strap is probably the best way of getting rid of the problem. A piece cut from a bicycle puncture repair patch, superglued to the strap, is often enough.

If you don't feel confident working with the delicate hard disk then take it to a specialist, the cost shouldn't be too high. Other than the grounding strap there is little physical preventative maintenance that can be done by the average user to a hard disk. Data maintenance is covered in other chapters.

Head Actuators

The Actuator is the device that moves the heads to the required location on the hard disk. There are only two types in current usage. These are Voice Coil and Stepper Motor. As a general rule of thumb Stepper Motors are fitted to drives that are less than 80 Mb capacity, have an access time greater than 40 milli seconds or are low cost devices. Voice Coil Actuators are fitted to drives of greater than 80 Mb capacity, have an access time of 28 ms or less and are generally higher priced units.

The foregoing paragraph is substantially correct at the time of writing but, as more and more hard disks are manufactured, the techniques required to make Voice Coil Actuators is improving and the cost is dropping to within 30% of the cost of a Stepper Motor. We expect that the Stepper Motor Actuator will all but have disappeared within the next two or three years.

Stepper Motor Actuators

One of the problems with Stepper Motors is their inherent inaccuracy. Because they are a mechanically linked system they can only move one track at a time and they are very prone to temperature changes. Over the past couple of years there has been a classic example of the foibles of Stepper Motors.

A British manufacturer, noted for its range of PC clones, was having a great deal of trouble with the hard disk drives fitted to its computers. Both the drive units fitted by the company and units supplied by many after market companies suffered from 'Monday Morning Boot Failure Sickness'. When the computer was first switched on in the morning, the machine would fail its POST, i.e. Power On Self Test, and report a '1701' error and then sit and look blankly at the operator.

As a supplier of both this type of computer and a range of hard disk kits, we as a company got involved. For weeks we sat and pondered as to what the problem might be. There seemed to be no common factor. It did not seem to matter what part of the country the machine was being used in whether it had been off for 6 or 16 hours.

The light began to dawn when we read a snippet in an old technical journal that recommended formatting the hard disk in the environment in which it was to be used. The penny dropped - the problem was temperature related. The disk drive had been low level formatted in a nice warm office or shop and sent to the customer. He had then put the machine into an office with some form of central heating. Being a canny chap the heating was switched off at night and over the whole weekend.

The fall in temperature and hence the contraction in size of the hard disk platters was sufficient to throw the whole drive slightly out of kilter and thus the stepper motor was unable to find track 0 and hence the boot sector. If it cannot find the boot sector then the machine just stops. The problem was made worse because this particular manufacturer did not fit a fan to the system unit of this particular computer. The temperature in the system box could and frequently did rise to unacceptably high levels thus making the problem worse, because too high a temperature could make the platters expand with a similar result!

The cure was not simple but effective in most cases. We had to do the actual low level format in the place the computer was to be used, usually in the middle of the day. The user then had to try and arrange for the heating to be put on an hour earlier than normal. Failing that, switch the computer on for an hour or two before it was actually required and then reboot when it was completely warmed up. Oh yes, we also fitted a small fan in the system box! The solution, though inelegant, works.

Anyway, back to Stepper Motors. To transfer the motion of the motor to the drive heads, a split band technique is normally used. One end of a special steel alloy band is anchored to and passed around the shaft of the Stepper Motor. The band is wrapped round the head assembly and then to a sprung anchor point. As the motor moves the rotary motion is transformed into linear motion which moves the head assembly one step at a time. The sprung end acts as both a shock absorber to prevent overshoot and as a method of keeping the length of the band the same, no matter what the position of the head assembly.

Miniscribe did for a time use a Stepper Motor that converted rotary motion to linear motion by using a rack and pinion inside the hard disk enclosure. This used a small pinion gear on the shaft of the Stepper Motor connected to a rack on the head assembly. The arrangement had advantages in that is was more reliable and had greater physical and thermal stability. However the trade off was that the manufacturing tolerances required were much greater and the pinion gear and the rack tended to wear over a period of time which led to decreased accuracy and therefore decreased reliability. The rack and pinion also tended to be much noisier that the split band and many users found the noise somewhat off putting.

Voice Coil Actuators

Voice coil motors do not suffer from any of the foregoing problems. They work purely by 'electro-magnetic force', which means that they can move in steps of less than one track at a time and if the disk platter has expanded or contracted the electronics governing the motor can make it 'hunt' for the required track.

The whole head assembly in a voice coil drive is connected directly to the motor. The manufacturing process is somewhat simpler than Stepper Motors. The original idea for the Voice Coil Actuator came from the audio industry.

A loudspeaker works by having a cone of paper or similar material attached to a cylinder which has a coil wound round it. The cone is suspended in a cone shaped metal framework with a round permanent magnet attached to it. The coil slides over the magnet which is fixed in position. When an electric current is passed through the coil, it produces a magnetic field which interacts with the permanent magnet which it surrounds. The two magnetic forces make the coil and its associated cone of paper move, this vibrates the air in front of the cone and a sound wave is produced. The main point to realise is that there is no contact between the coil and the magnet and that there is therefore no mechanical linkage to induce errors.

One of the ways to determine whether or not a hard disk has a Voice Coil Actuator is from the number of heads. If this is an odd number then it is almost certainly a voice coil drive with a 'closed loop servo mechanism'. Another name for this type of drive is a 'Dedicated Surface' drive. The name occurs because one side of one platter is not used for ordinary data storage but instead it has the track numbers recorded on to it. The head on this surface is Read Only and therefore the track information cannot be erased or changed. The closed loop refers to the fact that the head on that surface feeds back its position to the Voice Coil Actuator electronics which then uses a 'feedback' loop to tell the Voice Coil Actuator when to start and stop moving the head assembly.

One very important point is that this type of mechanism is not affected by temperature change because the dedicated surface is telling the control electronics which track it is currently positioned over and not, as in a Stepper Motor, a counting chip telling the head assembly where it thinks the heads are. Also the dedicated surface will expand and contract at the same rate as the actual data surfaces. Normally the platter that contains the servo information will be in the middle of the stack of platters, this is the most stable point of the platter assembly during start up. Many modern drives are capable of recalibrating themselves at regular intervals whilst the drive is running. This can be disconcerting; you are sitting at the computer, not actually accessing the drive when all of a sudden it starts to make noises, as though it is working. The noise is similar to that which the drive makes when loading data. This is caused by the drive performing a recalibrate operation and is nothing to worry about. Other drives will also park themselves after a period of inactivity. This is particularly true of portable computers.

However, it is worth noting that VCA drives can and do have an even number of surfaces. Another major advantage of the Voice Coil Actuator is Automatic Head Parking. When the power is switched off, the head assembly is automatically pulled back to the 'safe' position by the spring assembly that the Voice Coil Actuator works against. The heads automatically unpark when the power is re-applied. It is worth noting that if you have a self parking drive that you should not use a 'park' program on it. The supplier of your drive should be able to tell you whether or not your drive is self parking.

Two types of Voice Coil Actuator are available, the Rotary and the Linear coil. The Rotary type has a coil which moves around a shaft which is surrounded by stationary magnets. The rotary motion is transmitted straight to the heads which are mounted on an arm attached directly to the coil. The movement produced is very similar to that made by the arm of a record player, i.e. the heads move in an arc. In the Linear Voice Coil Actuator the coil moves along a straight track, so the magnets are stationary. The movement is essentially a straight line. The more expensive drives tend to use the rotary Voice Coil Actuator.

Read/Write Heads

Each side of a platter will have its own Read/ Write head, i.e. between two platters there are two heads. The head is connected to the Actuator motor by an arm. The series of arms and heads form a single unit, so that all the heads move as one. Contrary to what many people think the heads do not touch the platters, except when there is no power to the drive. Once the drive is operating the heads effectively ride on a cushion of air so that they do not make contact with the magnetic coating. The gap between the head and the surface of the platter can be as little as 1/10 of a millionth of an inch.

This is the reason why you should always park the heads before moving the machine. Parking quite simply means moving the heads to an unused section of the disk and then locking them in place until power is re-applied to the drive. With the heads parked any jolt to the machine will cause the heads to crash only at this safe area. (A good park program, by the way, locks up the keyboard so that you can only restart the drive by turning off the power and then rebooting the machine.)

Logic Board

The Logic Board contains the electronics that makes the drive unit work, i.e. it controls the Spindle Motor and the Head Actuator. It also communicates with the Controller in an agreed standard. The logic board can be removed from the drive and replaced if necessary - however you may well find that the cost of a new logic board is higher than the cost of a new drive. Such are the foibles of Capitalism! When you are handling a drive unit you should try never to touch the exposed solder points on the back of the logic board. All the electronic components of a computer are very susceptible to stray magnetic and electrical currents. Your body can, and does, act as source of both of these. Although the levels may be very low they can still be strong enough to interfere with the fragile components, particularly if you touch the exposed pins or connection points.

Connectors and Cables

On an ST506 and ESDI interface drive there are two flat rectangular connectors, usually located at the back of the drive, with lines of gold coloured metal inlaid on them. One contains 17 strips, making 34 connections because there are two sides, and the other has 10 strips, with a total of 20 connections. If you look at the bottom of the logic board you can see through the coating and you will find that these strips are merely the ends of the circuitry. The larger of the two, the one with 34 pins, is the one used to daisy chain two drives together. This means that you can use one cable with two connector blocks to link two drives together to one controller. The connection is used to transmit instructions from the controller to the electronics of the drive, which then causes the head and motor to operate.

The smaller connector, the one with 20 pins, is the data connection. It is this that receives and transmits the signals containing the actual information that is to be written on the disk. The data connectors are never daisy chained: each drive must have a separate data cable and the controller always has two connections on it to allow this. Finally there is the power input. This is usually a hexagonal shaped slot which contains four pins. Into this is placed the female plug on the end of the four wires from the computer power supply. A general rule of thumb is that the smaller the platter size the lower the power consumption, i.e. there is less inertia to overcome.

IDE and SCSI drives only have two connectors, the power connector is the same as on the above drives. The data/control cable is completely different, IDE drives have a ribbon cable with 40 wires, of these 7 are grounds, 16 are data lines and the rest are control lines.

On some drives there may also be a grounding connector which is used to transmit the excess static to the body of the system unit. However most of today's modern machines use a mounting bay to which the drive is secured by four screws and these make the need for a grounding connector redundant. However it is still a good idea to use the ground connector if at all possible.

Bezel

The bezel is simply the plastic cover at the front of the drive, i.e. the bit that you can actually see once the drive has been installed. It usually has a line of ventilation holes and a single LCD light which comes on once the drive receives power.

Configuration Details

At the back of the logic board, or occasionally beneath it, is the point at which the drive configuration occurs. Normally these are preset by the manufacturers and they do not need to be changed by the user and should only be changed after careful reference to the manual supplied with the drive.

The first item is the Drive Select Jumper. This is used to choose the channel to which the drive will respond. The controller sends signals to the drive along one of two channels and each drive must be set to respond to a different channel; a single standard controller can control a maximum of two physical drives. If the computer has only one hard drive fitted then its drive must be configured to use Channel 1. Where there are two drives the one with the lowest designator, i.e. C:, uses the first channel and the other drive uses the second.

The final item is the Terminating Resistor. The purpose of this is simply to stop any signal going back up the cables to the controller. The Terminating Resistor must be placed on the first physical drive - not the second - because the controller acts through the first and this is the end of the line, as it were.

One last thing. Usually, the top of the drive unit will have a number of labels stuck on it. These give the model number and the manufacturer's warning about the warranty and finally a large label which contains details of any errors in the coating that the disk contains. For all that the manufacturing process of hard disk drives is very closely monitored at every point, it is not really possible to ensure that the coating is perfect, except in very expensive drives. The Error Map label tells you what Cylinder and Side of which platter(s) are damaged, and how large the imperfection is in terms of the number of bytes. This latter is somewhat curious because you would expect it to be given in terms of Kb or Sectors, until you realise that the formatting process, see later, does not use either of these terms but relies on bytes.

Hard Disk Types

All hard disks are basically the same, in that they contain the same basic elements as outlined above, but there are a number of different interfaces available and these affect a number of properties of the disks.

When it comes to adding a hard disk drive to your system you are limited to using those drives which operate with the same interface as you already have installed. It used to be difficult to add other controllers to an AT system, these days SCSI & AT interface drives will live quite happily together on the same data bus and it is now quite practical to have more than two hard disks on a system.

Theoretically, on an XT, you could have a hard disk which uses an MFM controller and then add a second hard disk using RLL encoding, with a second controller card. (The encoding scheme determines how efficient the recording of the information will be on the disk.) In practise fitting two controllers may lead to problems, before spending lots of money on a second drive and controller make certain you know that the two controllers can live together on the computer. If in doubt ask the supplier. If possible borrow and read the manual for the controller before you buy.

The original standard interface was the ST-506/412, created by Shugart Associates in the days when the man himself still ran the company. IBM used this interface on their original hard disk machine, the XT, and for a while there were no problems because any hard disk you wanted to install used the same controller and encoding procedure. Thus you could purchase any hard disk and connect it to the machine in the safe and sure knowledge that it would work. But that was in the early days and since then things have changed dramatically.

In fact first the controller used by IBM was the XEBEC 1210. This was an ST506/412 controller that used MFM encoding. MFM stands for Modified Frequency Modulation and it refers to a specific method of data encoding which is used to convert the digital signal from the computer into magnetic flux changes which will be used on the disk to store the data.

MFM used a fixed-length system and thus the pattern of bits it creates will always occupy the same space on the disk. As an encoding system it is very reliable but it does tend to require a large amount of linear space for any file. The reason has to do with the way it places the flux reversals. In MFM encoding these must always be clearly separate from each other and this in turn fixes the number of sectors per track that can be used. All MFM drives use 17 Sectors per Track for hard disks. The only way to increase the capacity of an MFM disk is to add more platters. As this is not very practical from an end user's point of view it means you have to add another drive to your system. (MFM encoding is also used for floppy disks by the way, because it is so reliable.)

An alternative method of data encoding is RLL which stands for Run Length Limited. Ideally the acronym should be followed by two digits as in

RLL 2,5, where the first refers to the minimum number of zero bits allowable between two 1's and the second digit refers to the maximum, i.e. the limit. The advantage of RLL is that it does not require fixed lengths and thus it is more efficient in terms of storage capacity. However the consequence is that it is not as reliable as MFM. In reality the two types are just as reliable at the end of the day, simply because the RLL controller is better than its earlier cousin. Using RLL means that the capacity of the disk can be increased significantly, by as much as fifty per cent, because it uses 26 Sectors per Track. A second advantage is that RLL drives are much faster at data transfer.

Another controller type is ESDI, which stands for Enhanced Small Device Interface, which at one time seemed to be becoming the new standard, but it has since almost vanished. It was created in 1983 by the Maxtor Corporation in the USA and was designed to work with both hard disks and tape drives. The advantage of it was that the encoder/decoder was built into the drive unit itself, rather than into the controller as with MFM and RLL, and this made it very fast. The transfer rate of an ESDI drive can be anything up to a maximum of 3 megabytes a second - phenomenally fast - although it is more usual to have transfer rates of around half that.

Most ESDI drives use 34 Sectors per Track which gives a further significant increase in data capacity on the same disk. In addition most ESDI drives use 1:1 interleaving which further enhances their speed. The ESDI system is found on most PS/2 machines as it was adopted by IBM as the new standard interface. Unfortunately ESDI interfaces tend to be expensive and so they were only taken up by the manufacturers of high cost machines.

The final interface covered here (IDE rates a complete chapter later on) is SCSI or the Small Computer Systems Interface - usually referred to as Scuzzy. This has actually been around for a long time, eight years or so, in various forms. Originally it was developed by Shugart Associates who decided to develop an interface that would be capable of interfacing with everything. The idea was certainly attractive, and so they set about designing it. What they came up with was something called the Shugart Associates System Interface. Wanting to get it adopted as a standard they applied to the American National Standards Institute to have it accepted. As with all bureaucratic organisations ANSI wanted changes made and refinements and so on. Shugart accordingly made these and the device was given approval but its name was changed to Small Computer System Interface. (One industry rumour says that this is the real reason why Shugart Associates changed their name to the Shugart Corporation. Think about it!)

The thing about SCSI is that it is not a disk interface at all - it is a system level interface and is usually applied directly at the motherboard level. In other words it is not really a controller. You need to use a card called the Host Adaptor to be able to get at it and this allows you to connect several peripherals, including disk drives, printers, scanners, tape streamers and the like, together so they can communicate effectively and rapidly. The advantage of the system is that you can then use up to eight separate controllers into a single system and have them all communicate with each other without having to constantly change data from one form to another. In practice you can only connect seven devices to one controller because the controller itself is a SCSI device and is always there! In effect it is like having a network contained within a single machine with all the devices integrating together into a cohesive whole. You can use either ST506/412 or ESDI controllers with SCSI. However if you do, the ST506 will normally always 'sign on' first. This means that this is the drive the computer will 'boot' from, i.e. load the operating system from.

At the time of writing the original of this book, the only manufacturer who had implemented SCSI in a big way was Apple but that is changing. IBM has now adopted SCSI instead of ESDI and future machines will use it. Most optical disk systems, including CD-ROM, use SCSI and more and more standard type peripherals now have an SCSI interface. Most other manufacturers now offer a SCSI interface option, particularly where very large, i.e. up to 2.8 Gigabyte drives are required. In fact the one major reason why SCSI is really going to take off is because of CD-ROM and Multimedia.

As well as the interface differences there are a huge number of different sized hard disks available. The list of them is far too long to include here - we do have such a list and it fills more than 80 A4 pages. The up-to-date list is included on the software disk that can be purchased to accompany this book. (See details at the front of the book.) What follows is only a partial listing of the main ones. Disk drives are created to a specific standard and each has a distinct number. In addition there are manufacturing differences between MFM and RLL drives - you cannot simply change controller and increase the disks storage capacity. Within each drive there are a different number of platters, and thus heads, and each therefore produces a different number of cylinders.

Below is a list of 'standard disk' types, taken from the C-MOS setup of a typical AT type machine.

Drive No.	Cyl's	Heads	Write	Land-Zone
01	306	04	128	305
02	615	04	300	615
03	615	06	300	615
04	940	08	512	940
05	940	06	512	940
06	615	04	NONE	615
07	462	08	256	511
08	733	05	NONE	733
09	900	15	NONE	901
10	820	03	NONE	820
11	855	05	NONE	855
12	855	07	NONE	855
13	306	08	128	319
14	733	07	NONE	733
15	306	04	128	306
16	612	04	NONE	663
17	977	05	300	977
18	977	07	NONE	977
19	1024	07	512	1023
20	733	05	300	732
21	733	07	300	732
22	733	05	300	733
23	306	04	NONE	336
31	1024	08	512	1024
32	615	06	NONE	615

Drive No.	Cyl's	Heads	Write	Land-Zone
33	1024	11	NONE	1024
34	925	09	NONE	925
35	809	06	128	852
36	781	02	NONE	805
37	781	04	NONE	805
38	781	06	NONE	805
39	805	04	NONE	805
40	1024	05	512	1024
41	1024	08	NONE	1024
42	1024	09	NONE	1024
43	820	06	NONE	820
44	960	09	NONE	960
45	830	10	NONE	830
46	1024	15	NONE	1024
47	981	05	NONE	981

{Types 24 to 30 are not used. Table courtesy of Tandon plc}

On modern machines you probably find types 48 and 49 which are 'User Definable', this means exactly what it says, the user can type in the values that his drive type requires, e.g. 1674 cylinders x 16 heads x 54 sectors per track. This would be for a drive with a capacity of 723 Megabytes.

The table is derived from a so called standard list produced by IBM some years ago. A BIOS from a different manufacturer may well have a slightly different table, particularly from number 15 on. For the most part, so long as your drive is listed in the table, it doesn't matter where it is in the table. Of course there have to be exceptions and there are two, both very important under certain circumstances.

Firstly, all SCSI host adaptors have an on-board micro processor with associated ROM containing driver software, SCSI are NOT installed in the drive table, you tell the C-MOS setup program that no hard disk is installed! Don't worry, at boot time the computer's boot program interrogates INT55h and finds the SCSI controller which then takes over as far as the hard disk is concerned.

Secondly, NOVELL netware. NOVELL is the de facto standard networking system throughout the world, others do exist but NOVELL probably has 70% of the installed networks. It is a very good system in many ways but does have one massive failing, it can only use drives that either can be installed in the drive table between numbers 1 to 47 (early versions of Novell could on use the first 15 entries) or have a specially written piece of 'driver' software. When you are reading the section on IDE drives, you will notice that many of these drives do not follow normal drive table rules and are therefore unsuitable for use on a NOVELL network unless you follow certain rules. If you are installing either a new drive in to a NOVELL network, or install a NOVELL network, please read the manuals very carefully before you begin otherwise you may lose data!

ESDI drives are also a bit of a special case. They are always installed as drive type 1. They contain a special bit of software which fools the operating system into thinking that they are a 10 megabyte drive until they are up and running, when their true size shows.

Fitting a drive

Once you have purchased the drive unit, having determined the interface and controller you want to use, the drive capacity, etc., fitting it is simplicity itself - although what happens thereafter depends on the make of your machine. You should have the following items:

The drive unit itself,
Two ribbon cables, a wide 34-pin one and a narrow 20-pin one (ST506 or ESDI) or 1 ribbon cable (SCSI or IDE drive),
A controller card,
A manual of some description and possibly software on a floppy disk.

To fit the drive unit you will need a Philips head screwdriver, preferably a long shafted one because it is easier to use, and patience. This latter is the most important item of all! One vital thing that must be done is to READ THE MANUAL before you start. I know manuals are boring and generally awkward to use and most of them are badly written but.... please do read it before you go any further. The manual contains a multitude of information about the drive and the associated software (if any) and it is actually worth your while to read it. After all, you are going to be using the device for some time and so you might as well learn everything you can about it before you start. So make yourself a cup of coffee, find a comfortable chair and sit down.

Read the manual from cover to cover, skimming it if necessary, but make sure you get all the salient facts about the drive before you start.

90% of problems with computers would not exist if people bothered to read manuals!

Then, turn off the power to the machine and preferably unplug it completely. Clear the desk so that you have enough room to work and then open the system box. This usually necessitates removing a number of screws from the back of the box and then sliding off the casing. On some machines this is very easy; on others it is a pain in the neck.

Decide which of the vacant slots the controller will sit in and then remove the associated dust cover at the back of the machine. Place the controller into the guides and position it over the slot. Push it down firmly but don't force it. By the same token make sure you are using the correct type of slot. On my AT the controller has two flanges and therefore it needs a sixteen bit slot - it won't go into an 8-bit one. Equally don't put an 8-bit card into a 16-bit slot. Be careful, when handling the controller, to hold it by the edges and try not to touch the gold edge connectors .

When fitting an IDE or SCSI drive please ignore references to TWO ribbon cables and substitute ONE ribbon cable.

Now connect the two ribbon cables to the controller. Generally, they will only fit one way so if they don't slide on easily, don't force them. Make sure you have them right way round and use firm but gentle pressure.

Remove the drive unit from its packing, without touching the exposed solder points, and connect the other end of the ribbon cables to it. Next, take one of the free power lines and connect this to the drive unit, again making sure it is the right way round. Then carefully sit the drive on top of the open system box, preferably on top of the carrier.

Reconnect the machine to the power and turn it on. All you are doing at this stage is checking that the drive works. The LED at the front of it should light up and you should be able to hear the drive spinning. Give it time because it needs to reach 3,600 RPM. If the drive has been pre-formatted and had the system installed then your machine may boot up directly from it - if it doesn't then don't worry, yet. Once you are sure the drive is working satisfactorily, turn off the power again and remove the mains plug.

Disconnect the power supply and the ribbon cables from the drive unit and then put it safely to one side. Put it down carefully because the heads are not now parked. Ideally put it on top of the packing it came in. Have a look at the carrier, the bit that holds the floppy drive unit and where you will put the new hard drive. These vary a bit from manufacturer to manufacturer, but you should find that there are two screws down each side holding the existing drives and a blanking piece. This latter is simply a bit of shaped metal that covers a vacant slot in the carrier.

Remove the screws from this, putting them within reach, and then slide the blanking piece out through the front of the carrier. Don't bash it on any existing drive, slide it straight out - it should move without any real force.

Pick up the hard drive and slide it into the now accessible slot. Reconnect the ribbon cables and the power supply. This is generally a bit fiddly and will make you wish you had tentacles instead of fingers. Take your time and make sure they are connected correctly.

Now, whilst holding the drive in roughly the right position with one hand, replace the screws you took out earlier. Ideally you want to put in diagonally opposite screws, in order, but it doesn't really matter as long as you hold the drive in place until they are all in.

Tidy up the cables - you usually find that they have to be draped over existing cards and then tucked around them to make the sit comfortably. Replace the casing - making sure you don't trap any of the cables - and secure it again. Reconnect the mains and turn the machine on again. What happens next depends on your machine. With some PC's you need do nothing, other than format the disk if necessary, while with the majority you have to identify the drive first through a SETUP program.

The Setup is a special program that holds the information about what devices are installed, the time, date, etc. How it is accessed depends on the BIOS manufacturer. It is rare these days to find a computer with a disk based setup program, on most modern computers it is contained in the BIOS. Most computers that have a PHOENIX BIOS fitted will allow the setup program to be accessed by pressing the CTL+ALT keys together and while keeping them pressed, press the S key. This will not work if you have run any type of KEYBOARD program. Many machines will allow you to run the setup during the boot up. Reference to the motherboard manual will usually tell you how.

Whichever method is used, you will normally be presented with a menu type screen onto which you can identify the new disk, generally by toggling between the various types of disks that can be run on that machine. The drive type number is the important part that the computer needs although some machines will not allow you to use certain types of disk. Again, the important thing is to read the manual that accompanied your computer - there are so many clones and compatibles that it is simply not possible to give details of how each one is set up.

Hard Cards

From our experience in selling computers and related peripherals, and from reading through the computer magazines, it has become very apparent that there is a great deal of confusion over what a Hard Card actually is. Hence the inclusion of this section of the book.

If you have read through the preceding chapters and sections of this book you will already have a good understanding of what a hard disk and controller cards are, and what the function of each is. A Hard Card is, quite simply, the combination of the two into a single 'organism'. The hard disk element is mounted onto a metal back plate which contains the controller and all the necessary cables and connections - all built in to it.
The actual hard disk is no different from any other hard disk of the same capacity. The only proviso to a hard card is that the mechanism is almost always a 3.5-inch unit. A 30 Mb hard card contains 3.5-inch platters, enclosed in the necessary air-tight box, bonded to the back plate. At the other end is fitted the correct controller card and connecting the two are the cables. The only different requirement for the controller card is that it must have some form of power output for the hard disk. This is normally provided in the form of a 6 pin connector. The controller merely collects +5v and +12v from the host computer's bus and acts as a transfer adaptor to the hard disk mechanism.

The major difference is that a Hard Card is self contained and can often be fitted in a matter of seconds, you simply push it into a vacant slot on the machine; a hard disk, controller and cables on the other hand are usually a little more difficult to fit.

Once upon a time, hard cards were made in 20 Mb and 30 Mb units. Nowadays, as larger capacity 3.5-inch form factor drives become available, higher capacity hard cards are appearing. At the time of writing, the largest is a unit with a formatted capacity of 200Mb. No doubt as the technology improves, manufacturers will squeeze more and more on to the 3.5-inch form factor drive and hard cards will be available in much greater capacities.

In essence you can use a hard card in the same way as a normal hard disk i.e. you can store software and data on it, remove it and then place it into another machine and use it there - but it is much more awkward. Normally you would fit a hard card to a single machine and then leave it in place.

Their primary disadvantage is that they are of fixed size; if you want to increase your storage you have to install another hard card, or better still a complete hard disk system, and that uses up the available slots rather quickly.

Chapter 4
IDE Drives

WARNING: Never attempt to perform a low level format of an IDE drive. It can be fatal to your data and the drive itself.

IDE stands for Integrated Drive Electronics. Integrated means that, like SCSI drives the actual interface between the drive and the computer is contained on the drive itself. The electronics on the drive are also intelligent and are capable of very sophisticated management of the flow of data to and from the drive and of the way the drive is organised at 'low level', more of this later.

The manufacturers' reasons for developing IDE were mainly economic although from the users point of view there are two distinct benefits to be gained from the IDE drives. A trade off is that there are a couple of disadvantages to an IDE drive. However neither of the disadvantages are bad but ones that you need to be aware of, both will be discussed later in the chapter.

The benefits

Firstly there is the economic benefit, IDE has been exceptionally quick to gain popular acceptance. This is mainly due to computer manufacturers fitting them to new PCs. The result has been that the drives are being manufactured in very large numbers. This cost benefit is being passed on to the end user who is seeing greatly reduced prices for the drives. At the time the first edition of this book was being written, i.e. November 1989, a 20 megabyte Seagate ST225 drive, which had an access time of 65ms, was being sold at a retail price of around £210.00 plus interface. A suitable interface for an AT would have cost in the region of £90.00, thus the total cost would be around £300.00. The ST225 is an MFM drive and as such has a maximum data transfer rate of 5 megabits per second. In practice the fastest that could be achieved with this drive was in the region of 160 K byte, that is 1.47 megabits per second.

Because of the computer manufacturer's acceptance of the IDE principle, many main boards now come with an IDE interface built on to the main board. At the current time of writing, December 1991 a 20 Mb ST125A is widely advertised at £130.00 and most modern computers would not require an interface card. If an interface card is required one would need to spend about £20.00. Thus the total cost is around £150.00! Incidentally the interface card would normally also include a floppy disk drive controller, two serial ports and a parallel port. There may even be a 'games' port on the same card!

In addition to the cost benefit there is also the benefit of speed. The example quoted above, the Seagate ST125A, has an average access time of 28ms, in other words it is 2.5 times faster than the old ST238R. The data transfer rate is potentially much faster. Another advantage is that the drive consumes much less electrical power. This means that the computer power supply is not being run at anywhere near design limitations and that as the drive requires less power there is less heat to be dissipated. All this should mean that the computer's overall reliability is enhanced. The main reason that the drives are much cheaper to manufacture lies in the way the drives actually work.

The old ST506 interface relied on the hard disk controller card to do all the low level formatting and bad track management. It also looked after the flow of data to and from the drive. All the drive had to do was respond to the commands to it from the host computer and either accept data or send data back to the controller. The controller card then looked after the data separation and onward transmission to the data bus.

On the IDE drive that is all handled by the electronics on the drive. The drive has its own on board micro computer, in much the same way as an SCSI or ESDI drive does. In fact many people consider that the IDE drive are a bastardised form of the SCSI and ESDI interfaces. This is one reason why the IDE interface cards are so cheap. They are not interface cards in the old ST506 sense of the word. They merely act as a pathway for the commands from the operating system and the data stream to and from the drive.

The first thing the user should be aware of with an IDE drive is that on no account should any attempt be made to perform a low level format on it. In fact there are very few programs available that will perform a true low level format on an IDE drive but if you do have one that will actually do what the drive understands as a low level format, you stand every chance of damaging the drive beyond home recover/repair. There are certain programs on the market that may appear to be performing a low level format, even down to doing a head/cylinder count, just as you would expect to see on an ST506 or SCSI drive. In fact what you are seeing is the intelligent electronics telling the software porkies!

Why shouldn't you attempt to do a low level format? Why can it damage the drive beyond the point which some software can attempt to repair it if damage is done? To understand this is also to understand why the drives are cheaper to manufacture.

As previously discussed, the manufacturing process of the platters involves some very sophisticated polishing and deposition of plating media. Before the advent of the IDE drives, there were quality control checks which would reject a platter if it contained a larger percentage of bad tracks than 1 per surface (this was the figure used by Seagate, other manufacturers used different parameters). The HDA is then assembled and the complete hard disk is tested again. You will have seen the label on most hard disks that shows the 'Bad Track List'. Most manufacturers would reject a drive that showed more than one bad sector per megabyte of disk space, i.e. if a Seagate ST238R, which has a formatted capacity of 32 megabytes was tested and found to have 32 (or less) bad sectors it would be released for sale. However if it tested with 33 bad sectors it would be rejected as scrap and be returned to the production area for reworking.

With IDE drives, that has all changed. To digress for a moment, most manufacturers try and tell you something with the code numbers that they use for their drives. For example Seagate used to use a three or four digit number for all their drives, e.g. ST4096, ST238R, ST225, ST138A.

If you knew the code you could work out the drive size and interface. ST means 'Seagate Technologies' and is normally used to signify that the drive requires an ST506 interface. The first digit signifies the form factor, i.e. the physical size of the drive. 4 = 5.25" full height, 2 = 5.25" half height, 1 = 3.5" half height. The next two or three digits show the unformatted capacity of the drive, hence 096, means that the drive has an unformatted capacity of 96 megabytes. Therefore the Seagate ST4096 is a full height 5.25" drive with an unformatted capacity of 96 megabytes.

The last letter is used to show whether the drive is certified for use as an RLL drive. The absence of a last letter shows that the drive is an MFM type. The IDE drives will have a code that ends with the letter A, e.g. ST157A.

Seagate produce an RLL disk drive with an unformatted capacity of 57 megabytes, the ST157R. When formatted with the appropriate RLL controller the formatted capacity of this drive is 49megabytes. It can be easily worked out that there is a loss of approximately 17% of the unformatted capacity whilst the drive is being formatted. This space is not actually lost - is used to hold all the house keeping information that the interface needs to know which sector is which, what the sector size is and so on.

Seagate also produce an IDE drive, the ST157A which uses the identical HDA but has an IDE interface built in to the drive. The interesting thing is that the ST157A has a formatted capacity of 44 Megabytes. So does this mean that the IDE drive has a much greater house keeping overhead than the equivalent RLL device? The answer to that question is NO.

The reason for the apparent loss of capacity is very simple but shows one of the great advantages of the IDE drive to the user and the manufacturer at the same time. The bad track label on an IDE drive will NEVER have any entries in it! The missing 5 megabytes have gone to make sure that as far as the user is concerned bad tracks are a thing of the past with IDE drives. This sounds to good to be true and in fact it IS too good to be true!

Instead of IDE drives being manufactured to a higher standard, they are actually manufactured to a LOWER standard than their MFM or RLL equivalents! This does not mean that the customer is getting a raw deal, far from it.

The IDE drive has all the electronics required to control it actually on the drive, i.e. the printed circuit board, usually on the bottom of the drive, contains everything that used to be on the old interface card that all the other types of interface required. The IDE interface card that is fitted to the computer, either as a plug in-card or on the motherboard, is purely needed to pass commands and data to and from the computer to the drive. The interface card no longer has to translate the BIOS requests into something that the drive can understand.There is no need for a data separator on the interface card. All that is now handled by the electronics on the drive.

We have already said that there is a microprocessor on the drive, it has several functions. Firstly it is used to process the BIOS requests from the host computer to the drive, it controls the movement of the heads across the platters, keeps the motor spinning at the correct rate and sundry other things that the drive has to do. Its second function is to manage the bad track list, yes there are bad tracks on an IDE, in fact size for size, there are probably MORE bad tracks on an IDE drive than there are on an equivalent MFM, RLL, ESDI or SCSI drive!

So why is it that the user doesn't see any bad tracks? Quite simply when the drive is manufactured and checked, the bad tracks are mapped out as usual but instead of being written out on the label on top of the drive, they are written to specially reserved track(s) on the drive itself. These tracks are called 'engineering tracks'. This is not the only use for engineering tracks. A couple of tracks on the drive are cheaper than a ROM. More importantly they are smaller than a ROM and don't use any electrical power. On some drives the engineering tracks are used to store the software that controls the on-board micro. Where this approach is used, the software is usually uploaded at boot time, to a small static RAM. This may even be part of the actual micro chip which will also normally contain the small, (50 bytes or thereabouts) bootstrap program.

If a sector is found to be bad, the location is written to the engineering track and a spare sector is used to replace the bad sector. The reason for the missing five megabytes is that it is reserved as spare sectors. The drive electronics are intelligent. If, when trying to write data to a particular sector, the drive gets a write failure more than a certain number of times, it will mark that sector as bad and use one of the spare sectors (which will then have new ID information placed in its header) and to all intents and purposes, there will still be no bad sectors on the drive. All this is done by the on board microcomputer, in real time or 'on the fly' and is totally transparent to the user and is not under the user's control.

The main reason that a low level format should not be done on an IDE drive is that it would destroy the engineering tracks, the bad track list would be lost, as would, on some drives, the software that controls the on board micro! No software = no drive! So be warned, never be tempted to try and do a low level format on an IDE drive; you are quite likely to wind up with a drive that simply will not work, and whatever you do with whatever software tools you have at your disposal you will be totally unable to repair it. It really is a factory job to sort out, believe me, I know - I was the idiot who tried!

As previously stated, there is one program that I know of that can bypass the low level security of most IDE drives and will do a low level format. It will be disastrous to the drive. Most of the programs that perform low level formats on RLL, MFM, ESDI and SCSI drives will appear to do a low level format on an I.D.E drive. What happens is that the on-board micro is programmed to look for the type of commands that these programs, e.g. On Track 'Disk Manager', issue to the drive controller.

If they recognise such a command they go in to a 'lets fool the formatting software' mode and they will tell the software that they are performing the low level format; they may even show the correct response on the screen and you may be able to hear the drive stepping, just as though it is doing a proper low level format. In fact nothing is happening except that the drive is responding to the 'step' command. The problem is that the drive electronics are not intelligent enough, in most cases, to stop the partition information and/ or the FAT to be over written. So even just trying one of these programs can be sufficient to destroy all data on the drive with the disastrous results that can entail.

However not all software is as well behaved as Disk Manager, so may go in to the drive BIOS at a low level and whilst they don't do a true low level format, they do over write all the sectors with a big fat '0'; this means that your programs and data are no more! The moral of the story is DON'T DO A LOW LEVEL FORMAT even as an experiment. YOU HAVE BEEN WARNED.

One of the problems with IDE drives is that they are 'sector orientated'. The old ST506 drives were no problem to the BIOS of an AT type computer. The setup program in all ATs has a list of drive types from which the user chooses the one that is appropriate for the drive that is being installed in the computer. The drive tables normally contain 44 or 46 entries and list all the 'characteristics' of the drive. However the number of entries and the type of information that they show, (as distinct to what they contain), varies from BIOS to BIOS.

The chapter of the book is being written on a 386-33 clone of unknown manufacture but it has a

PHOENIX BIOS which has a help screen available during SETUP, one can simply press the F1 key to get a list of drive types up on the screen.

To go back to the example of the ST225, on almost all known setup programs, the ST225 would be a type 2. This is a standard 615 cylinders by 4 heads and formatted with 17 sectors per cylinder (track). The same drive type would also be perfectly suitable for the ST225A. However if a user requires to fit an ST1144A to a machine there is going to be a problem. The published figures for the drive show that it should be installed with 552 cylinders, 10 heads and is formatted with 36 sectors per track. Almost no setup program will have a drive type that comes anywhere close. There are several solutions to this problem.

Firstly, if the user has an old machine then use the drive type that comes closest to the formatted capacity of the drive, in the case of the ST1144A, with its formatted capacity of 96 megabytes, the type that may well be nearest is type 38, this is a 69 megabyte drive. However the user will only get a usable 69 megabytes of space from his shiny new 96 megabyte drive! With the older machine and no software to trick the BIOS, there is nothing else that can be done.

However the supplier of the ST1144A should have also supplied a copy of ON TRACK's 'Disk Manager' with the drive. This is a suite of programs which will help with this type of problem on older machines. Disk Manager is available commercially but is also supplied with larger, i.e. 40 Megabyte and above, Seagate drives. The copy that Seagate package with the drive will be specific for that particular family of drives and extreme caution should be used if it is used on any other drive. It will normally have a message showing that is was specially made for Seagate and when it is used will have the ST114A in its own drive table. For detailed instructions on the use of Disk Manager and Speedstor, please see the next chapter.

There is another way of dealing with the problem on an older machine and that is to change the BIOS. This is a fairly easy job to do; the BIOS is normally contained on two ROMs on the computer's motherboard. For further details on this approach please refer to the chapter dealing with BIOS. If the user is lucky and has a later machine he will actually be able to tell the setup program what his drive's apparent characteristics are.

The reason for saying apparent characteristics is that IDE drives are not like ST506, SCSI or ESDI drives. These drives are governed by their physical characteristics, i.e. they have a fixed number of cylinders, heads and sectors. These figures are certified by the manufacturer and with a few exceptions are the ones used in the BIOS drive tables.

IDE drives do not follow this convention. Instead they are certified to have a certain number of sectors. Within certain limitations, so long as this number is not exceeded, the user may set up whatever drive table entries he likes. For instance, the ST1144A has 223114 sectors certified. So long as the number of tracks x heads x sectors does not exceed this number, the user may use any parameters he wishes.

However, there are some restrictions. Most BIOS's will have problems if the numbers of tracks is greater than 1024. Seagate also put a limitation on the drive, that the number of heads times the number of sectors must not exceed 512. They publish a list of suggested BIOS entries, this is contained on the companion disk to this book. These have been tried on a variety of machines and found to give the best performance and it is probably wise to use these as a starting point.

ZBR or Zone Bit Recording

Some time ago it was realised that the system used to write sectors to the drive was somewhat wasteful. If you look at the diagram of the way and try to imagine that the tracks are laid out in a straight line, you will see that a sector on track 1, i.e. the outside one, has a much greater linear length than a sector on track 500, the inside one, yet both sectors store exactly the same amount of information. The actual length of the sectors can be worked out very easily using π. The calculation is ((π*d)/n) where d is the diameter of the track in question and n is the number of sectors per track.

If we use a 3.5" drive as a example then:

> Track 1 has a diameter of 3" and 17 sectors per track. 3.142*3=9.426". 9.426/17=0.5544". Therefore, if a sector holds a normal 512 bytes, each byte occupies.001".
>
> But track 500 has a diameter of 2" and the same 17 sectors per track. 3.142*2=6.284". 6.284/17=.37". The sector also has 512 bytes, each occupies .0007"

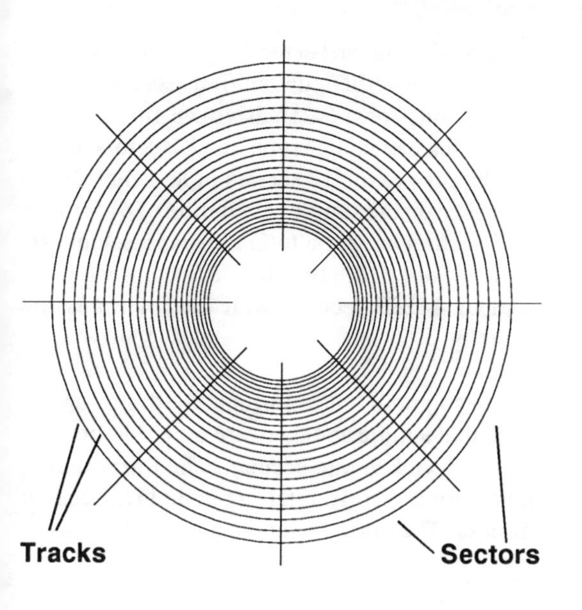

The difference is nearly 30%. This is wasted space! All the above calculations are done for an MFM drive. If we then consider a drive using the SCSI interface, we would have to recalculate everything because the standard on such a drive is 36 sectors per track.

The advent of drives with their own on-board microprocessors and controlling software led to the implementation of Zone Bit Recording. A drive utilising ZBR has the disk platter divided into zones, most systems use three but there can be as many as fifteen. Essentially each zone is treated as a different drive, in as much as the number of sectors per track is different.

So it is quite possible to have a 3.5" drive with an inner data diameter of 2.5" which has 36 sectors, the linear sector length on this drive is.22". If we then do similar sector length calculations for a 5.25" drive we find that the outer track has enough room for 72 sectors. Quite a difference to the 17 sectors of an MFM drive. If we then do the simple calculation of 615 tracks x 17 sectors we get a total of 10455 sectors. If we work out 615 tracks by 72 Sectors we get a total of 44280 sectors, well over 4 times the capacity.

So far so good, but unfortunately things aren't quite that simple and there are other factors that have to be taken into account. The linear length of a sector is merely a starting point in the design process. The other factors that have to be taken into account are the rotational speed of the drive, the angle of the head to the drive surface, the speed at which the electronics can work and the rate at which the data can be processed by both the drive and the computer data bus and memory.

Without going into very lengthy explanations there are also the considerations of the angle of attack of the head to the platter, the latency of the media and the settling time to name but a few. What ZBR actually does is provide the drive manufacturer with the best possible compromise that his designers can come up with to balance all the considerations against each other and give a very worth while increase in both capacity and speed. Speed, both in terms of the drive and data transfer rates.

Not least of the problems that ZBR brings with it, is that of translation. When a drive has a number of zones with different numbers of sectors in each, then the computer to which it is fitted has to be fooled in to thinking that it is dealing with something that it can understand, usually based around the 17 sector per track figure. Although some modern BIOS systems are capable of dealing with almost anything the manufacturer can produce, other BIOS will have major problems. One way out of this dilemma is to use the ubiquitous on-board micro to do the job of translating the physical sector patter in to a virtual or literal sectoring system. Because of the speed at which all this works it needs a dynamic real time management system, just the thing for an on-board micro processor to do. One manufacturer told us that the processing power on their latest 1.8 gigabyte drive was the equivalent of an 80286 running at 12Mhz!

One of the problems that IDE, SCSI and ZBR lead to is that the computer upon which they are being used is no longer in total control. Whilst you are using the machine for its ordinary day to day tasks, this does not present any problem. The problems arise when you want to use something like a de-fragmenter of a program to test the speed of your drive. A disk 'compressor' or de-fragmenter is not much of a problem, Norton and PC Tools both have one and both work reasonable well, BUT, before you use any of them, BACK UP YOUR DISK. If they do make a mess at least you will have your backup — won't you?

Testing Hard Disk Drives

Almost any magazine you open will have something about the speed of hard disk drives, whether it's the access time or the data transfer rate. There are many factors that affect the speed of a hard drive and the same drive can vary in speed from one machine to another. Even between the same model of machine!

The authors can remember some years ago testing a new 32 megabyte hard card on a certain machine and getting an extremely good data transfer rate. We accepted the drive as being good enough for the company to stock. That company had a policy of not supplying a drive unless it had been low level formatted 'in-house' and we used the test machine do all the low level formatting on the first delivery of the new hard card.

We then fitted two or three of the cards to brand new machines and ran our standard tests. The results were disappointing to say the least! After a lot of experimentation we found that the drives performed extremely well when formatted with an interleave of 3:1 when formatted on the test machine, but required an interleave of 5:1 on the new machines. This led Tim to try and devise some tests that were a little more useful than the commercially available programs that checked the access time and data transfer rate. There are many commercial programs that will give an indication of a drives performance but they tend to use one track only and a fixed sector or group of sectors to do the testing. Whilst this can be useful when testing a group of drives on the same computer, it does tell you how the drive performs under day to day usage. There is no commercial software that we know of that can provide accurate speed testing for IDE drives and the same applies to most SCSI drives. Speed testing and drive evaluation is something Tim has spent a lot of time doing and he has designed a series of simple tests that don't care what the interface is. The design and use of these tests could easily take half this book up. For anyone who is interested some of the tests are on the companion disk available from the address listed at the front of the book.

IDE Drive Connectors

Pin Signal Number	Name
1	RESET
2	GROUND
3	DD7
4	DD8
5	DD6
6	DD9
7	DD5
8	DD10
9	DD4
10	DD11
11	DD3
12	DD12
13	DD2
14	DD13
15	DD1
16	DD14
17	DD0
18	DD15
19	GROUND
20	KEYPIN
21	DMARQ
22	GROUND
23	DIOW-
24	GROUND
25	DIOR-
26	GROUND
27	IORDY
28	SPSYNC
29	DMACK-
30	GROUND
31	INTRQ
32	IOCS16-

33	DA1
34	PDIAD
35	DA0
36	DA2
37	CS1FX-
38	CS3FX
39	DASP-
40	GROUND

Chapter 5 Organising the Disk

Low Level Format

XT computers do not have built in BIOS to enable them to control a hard disk directly. The XT must rely on the controller card to supply the BIOS and usually the low level formatter as well. Surprising: although there are many manufacturers of hard disk controllers, there are only a few variations on a theme when it comes to the way that the low level formatter is accessed.

Most controllers are factory preset to reside at Hex address C800 and the method of kicking the on-board ROM containing the BIOS is to boot up using MS-DOS on a floppy disk. Once the A-Prompt has appeared on screen, run the DEBUG program supplied with whatever version of MS-DOS you have - it is usually to be found on the second of the two disks that are supplied with the machine.

The most commonly used hard disk controllers are made by Western Digital. The method of low level formatting is the same whether the drive is a 20 Mb or 30 Mb. The method described below will work for the majority of controllers. However before doing anything, please check what your hard disk is fitted with and read the instructions supplied with the drive.

Warning: A low level format destroys information, once started it is too late - the data has gone forever. Ensure that you have backed up any and all data files before you start.

Having checked that the drive is properly backed up, boot the computer using MS-DOS. When the A-Prompt appears enter DEBUG. After a couple of seconds your screen will look like this:

DEBUG
A>-

Now type in **G=C800:5** and press **Enter**. Almost immediately a message will appear, with Western Digital controllers it will be very similar to this:

Western Digital Format Revision 2.7 c1987
Current Drive is C

Enter New or press RETURN

At this stage you will almost certainly be installing the first hard disk on your computer so press **Enter**. The Screen will now contain the message:

Current interleave factor is 3, enter new interleave or press RETURN

For an explanation of Interleave factors and their influence on data transfer rates, see Chapter 7. At this point either press **Enter** or type the new Interleave factor and then press it. The message on the screen will now read:

Are you dynamically configuring the drive? (Y/N)

What the controller is asking at this point is, are you going to partition this physical drive as one drive or do you want to partition it into two or more logical drives? This is a question only you can answer, there are pros and cons for leaving it as one drive or making it into two or more logical units. With a capacity of up to 32 Mb our advice would be to leave it as one drive. With a higher capacity drive you must split it into two or more drives, unless you are using MS-DOS 4.0. How you split the disk depends again on what you want to do with it once it is installed. As a general rule, the largest drive that can be fitted to an XT is 65 Mb this of course can only be split into two 32 Mb partitions.

To work out how to partition the drive requires some simple mathematics. If the drive has 615 cylinders and a capacity of 20 Mb then each cylinder stores approximately 32.5 Kb. Therefore, if you want a split of 12 and 8 Mb, the 12 first partition needs to be 369 cylinders. A similar calculation will easily give you the figures needed to partition a 32 Mb or a 40 Mb drive.

If you do want to partition the drive, answer **Y** and press **Enter**. The screen will fill with a whole series of questions. These can be ignored except for the number of cylinders and the number of heads, e.g. 615 4. The program will accept default values for the rest and the space between the 615 and the 4 is important. The next question that will appear is: **Are you virtually configuring the drive?**

Here is where the results of the maths is required, type in the number of cylinders you want for the first partition, e.g. 369. The response will then be:

Press return to format drive C with an interleave of 3

Press **Enter** and the message **Formatting.........** will appear on the screen. Depending on the drive, this will take up to 15 minutes, the average is about 4 minutes for a 20 Mb drive and 9 minutes for a 65 Mb.

When the formatting is finished, the screen should display **Format successful, insert system diskette in drive A and press any key**.

Do so and the computer will now reboot to the A-Prompt. The next step is to write partitions to the drive using FDISK.

Using an AT does not present you with the foregoing problems. The AT can access the BIOS directly and thus recognise the drive. Most AT's come with a program entitled SETUP which will allow you to low level format the drive much easier. The program is usually menu driven and it effectively holds your hand through the entire process. The low level format will either have been already done by the manufacturer, before the disk was shipped, or the SETUP program can do it for you. Either way it is a much simpler process using an AT.

FDISK

However, once a drive has been low level formatted, it is still not recognisable by the operating system which needs to know;

1) A way of telling the host system exactly what the disk is, e.g. the type, partitioning, etc.

2) What type of operating system it is using and where it is stored. There are other types of operating system beside MS-DOS that can be used, e.g. Unix, PICK or OS/2. However MS-DOS is by far the most common operating system in the world of personal computing.

In order to ascertain this information the operating system needs to write it into the Master Boot Record (MBR). This also provides the pointer to where the system starts, how much space it takes up, whether or not it is currently active and a signature that is unique to itself. All this information is necessary before the disk can be used by the operating system. The program which provides all this information is FDISK.

Before going any further we would like to give you a word of warning. Careless use of FDISK is one of the fastest ways to devastate a hard disk drive! When used on a newly formatted disk it's safe BUT if you go poking around with a disk that already has data on it and therefore by definition must already have partition information, it is very easy to lose some if not all your data. It is exceedingly rare that you will ever need to run FDISK - indeed we would go so far as to say that you should not even have it on your hard disk. Keep it on the backup floppy which contains your complete MS-DOS commands. We totally refuse to accept any responsibility for any and all damage that you may cause as a result of misusing the FDISK program.

One of the most important things FDISK does is to create the partitions for the disk. There are some basic rules about these:

No matter how many hard disks you have, of whatever size, you must have a primary partition on the system. The primary partition will always be assigned the letter C - no matter what physical drive it is on. If the drive or MBR for Drive-C dies, DOS will automatically reassign Drive-C to the second primary partition if there is one.

If there is more than one physical drive, the primary partitions on each drive will be allocated sequentially, C, D, E etc. When each physical drive has had its primary partition letter allocated, then it goes back to the first physical drive and starts to allocate the secondary partitions. The effect of this is, that on a two hard disk system, Drive-C will be on the first physical disk, Drive-D will be on the second physical disk, Drive-E and Drive-F will be on physical disk 1, i.e. with drive C, whilst Drive-G, Drive-H and Drive-I will be on the same physical disk as D.

When you run FDISK the first screen presented will look like this;

FDISK Options
Current fixed disk drive: 1
Choose one of the following:
1. Create DOS Partition
2. Change active partition
3. Delete DOS Partition
4. Display partition information

Enter choice: [1]

The above example is lifted directly from a computer formatted with MS-DOS 4.0, so your version may look slightly different, but the basic screen will be very similar. Notice that the 'Enter choice' option has defaulted to [1].

Select option 4 and this will now tell you how the disk has been partitioned:

Current fixed disk drive: 1

Partition	Status	Type	Size Mb	Used
C:1	PRI	DOS	31	75%
2	EXT	DOS	10	25%

Total disk space is 41 Mbytes

The Extended DOS Partition contains Logical DOS Drives.

Do you want to display the logical drive information (Y/N)..? [Y]

If you now press **Y** this will be displayed:

Display Logical DOS Drive Information

Drv	Label	Mbytes	System	Usage
D:	?	10	FAT12	100%

Total Extended DOS Partition size is 10 Mbytes

On a hard disk that does not have any partitions defined, the display will simply say No Partitions Defined.

Option 4 is the only safe part of FDISK. Anything else can cost you data! So having checked whether or not there is anything there, you can now make the decision as to the type of partition needed. There are so many versions of MS-DOS and PC-DOS around it is not practical to list all the options available, so we shall only describe the correct procedure for MS-DOS 3.3. If you are using any other version then read the MS-DOS manual that was supplied with the version of MS-DOS you are going to use. Change to the directory (or disk) that contains FDISK and run it, i.e. type in **FDISK** and press **Enter**. The first screen is this:

Fixed Disk Setup Program Version 3.30
(C)Copyright Microsoft Corp. 1987
FDISK Options
Current Fixed Disk Drive: 1
Choose one of the following:

1. Create DOS partition
2. Change Active Partition
3. Delete DOS partition
4. Display Partition Information
Enter choice: [1]

At the bottom of the screen you will see the **Enter choice** option already has **[1]** entered. Change this to option 4, the Display Partition Information, before doing anything else. Having established either that there is no existing partition, or that you really do want to get rid of all your data and do a new partition table, you can now go to Option 1. The **Esc** key will take you back to the opening menu. Select Option 1 and this will now be displayed:

Fixed Disk Setup Program Version 3.30
(C)Copyright Microsoft Corp. 1987

FDISK Options
Create DOS Partition
Current Fixed Disk Drive: 1

1. Create Primary DOS partition
2. Create Extended DOS partition

Select Option 1 again and you get this:

Create Primary DOS Partition

Current Fixed Disk Drive: 1

Fixed Disk Space Available is 820 Cylinders

Use Maximum Allowed For DOS Partition (Y/N)

If you answer **Y** at this point, FDISK will allocate enough cylinders to create a 32 Megabyte partition. If you answer **N**, FDISK will ask you how many cylinders you want to use for this partition and to enter the start cylinder number. A rough guide to the number of cylinders to the size of partition ratio is easy to work out. Simply divide the number of cylinders by the total size of the drive in Megabytes, e.g. 820 cylinders divided by 40 = 20.5. In other words 20.5 cylinders = 1 Mb. If you want a partition of 22.5 Mb, multiply 20.5 by 22.5 and type in the result, i.e. 461.5. However, only whole numbers can be used so enter either 461 or 462.

Now for the peculiarity of FDISK under MS-DOS 3.3, the program will not now allow you to create another partition! You must first allow FDISK to reboot the computer. To create the second and subsequent (if required) partitions, run FDISK again and select option 1 followed by option 2. Then answer the questions regarding sizes as they appear on the screen.

The computer will once again reboot, the partition information is written to the disk as you tell FDISK how to do it, but the computer cannot recognise the hard disk until it reads it from the hard disk itself. Incidentally, this is the reason for the reboot after creating the first partition under MS-DOS 3.3; the extended partition information has to be written after the first partition has been established on the disk.

High Level Format

Before a computer can recognise any disk, it must be high level formatted. On a floppy disk this is simply called formatting but on hard disks it is slightly different.

If you have read the preceding chapters you will know that hard disks can store several different operating systems, and these must be stored in different places to prevent them getting mixed up and interfering with each other. This is one of the reasons for placing partitions on the hard disk. Different operating systems will almost certainly require different ways of storing their information on the disk, and this means that different types of format may need to be used. What the format command actually does is to alter the state of the magnetic flux to prepare it to store the data.

Low level formatting prepared the disk by placing a number of concentric rings on the surface of each platter, these are the Tracks. Each track was then subdivided into a number of sectors. Sectors will normally hold 512 bytes of information; this is true of all but a very few machines, which have a sector size of 1024 bytes.

The high level format has the task of preparing each sector for use by performing a number of different operations on it. The type and number of these operations depends on the type of drive and the operating system in use at the time. Most people reading this will only be interested in MS-DOS in one of its various forms so that is what we will describe.

The same program, FORMAT, is used for both hard and floppy disks. This immediately presents a danger, as it is very easy to accidentally type in FORMAT C: and erase all the data on Drive-C. There is a way of protecting against this; use the MS-DOS program LABEL to put a volume name on to the disk. FORMAT then checks for a volume label before it allows a format to proceed, simple but effective. One problem is that even if there is no label you are asked to supply confirmation of this before the formatting proceeds - and you cannot enter a blank label. Therefore any hard disk without a label cannot be formatted by MS-DOS!

So when you enter **FORMAT C:/S** what actually happens? Firstly, the media is scanned and each sector is identified and a unique number called a CHRN (Cylinder Head Record Numeric) is allocated to that sector. A timing mark is also given to each sector.

> 'Cylinder' is the actual cylinder identified in the range 0 to n, i.e. the maximum number on the surface.
>
> The 'Head' number is what identifies the platter that the sector is actually on.
>
> 'Record' is the sector itself. The first two elements, i.e. CH, enable the operating system to know where that sector is and the Record number is what gives each sector a unique identification.
>
> 'Numeric' is simply used to store the format type MS-DOS uses:

Numeric Value	Sector Size (Bytes)
0	128
1	256
2	512
3	1024

A typical CHRN series would be:

Cylinder	Head	Record	Numeric
001	0	0	3
01	0	1	3
01	0	2	3
nn	n	n	n
51	5	15	3
nn	n	n	n
612	5	9	3

The above table shows a series of typical entries for a disk drive which has at least 612 tracks (because 612 is the highest C number) 5 heads, and is formatted to the MS-DOS standard of 512 bytes per sector. Actually all the effort of numbering each sector is a complete waste of time as far as MS-DOS is concerned! MS-DOS does not bother about sector numbers at all. What the operating system does store is sector numbers - these are then stored in the FAT table which will discussed a little later. The real reason for numbering each sector is because that is the way the ROM BIOS works.

Imagine that you have a ball of string; you know where the ball starts but you cannot find the end because it is somewhere inside the ball. You need to mark the string so that someone else can use it to measure something. The logical way to do it is to measure a short length and tie a knot. Now you measure another equal length and tie two knots, next a third length and three knots and so on. In effect, the number of knots at any point tells you how many lengths you are from the beginning and is a rudimentary form of labelling. This is basically what the ROM BIOS does; it has a start point and measures off a sector which it identifies with the CHRN number, it then measures another sector and identifies that with the next CHRN number and so on until it reaches the end.

The sectors are then grouped together to form Clusters. A cluster is the smallest unit of measurement of physical disk capacity that MS-DOS can cope with. Clusters can be of various sizes, the usual is 4 sectors which form a cluster of 2048 bytes, i.e. 2 Kb of data. However, a 2 Kb cluster is not writ in stone. Older drives tended to have 4 Kb or 8 Kb clusters and some modern very high capacity drives can have similar sized clusters.

FORMAT does several other things in addition to marking each sector. Once this task is finished it writes the MBR or Master Boot Record. This is always the first sector on the first track or cylinder of the drive and contains such essential information as whether or not this is a 'bootable' drive, the type of format that has been used, the size of each cluster, where the boot programs are located, and so on.

The next job is to write the File Allocation Tables, which is followed by the Root Directory, that's the one that is at the very start of the drive. You will see it when you enter CD\. It usually contains COMMAND.COM and all the other programs such as CONFIG.SYS and AUTOEXEC.BAT. It will also contain all the first level directories. Part of the root directory on one of the computers that this book is :

[MS-DOS]	[JUNK]	[WINDOWS]
[S-BASE-4]	[WINWORD]	[DELTA]
[EXCEL]	[PPOINT]	[FLANCE]
[PSFONTS]	WIN.BAT	WS.BAT
WORK.BAT	X.BAT	Y.BAT
CONFIG.SYS	AUTOEXEC.BAT	

60 File(s) 11452416 bytes free

Some people may say that this has too many files in the root directory, certainly my co-author does. As a matter of interest, the more files there are in the root, the longer it takes to find any particular file. To get the above list, the command **DIR/W** was used, i.e. I told MS-DOS to give me a directory listing in wide format. This spreads the information across the screen in five columns. The more normal way to do it is just **DIR**, which produces a completely different way of displaying the files:

WIN	BAT	31	22-11-89	11:08p
WORKING	BAT	24	07-01-90	1:13p
WS	BAT	20	02-11-89	5:25p
X	BAT	39	26-09-89	5:30p
XTRA	COM	9627	09-07-89	9:17a

60 File(s) 11452416 bytes free

The major difference is that this time the files are listed showing their Size and Date & Time stamping. Each root directory entry occupies 32 bytes:

DESC	FORMAT	SIZE(BYTES)
Filename	ASCII Characters	8
Extension	ASCII Characters	3
Attributes	BIT Coded	1
Reserved	Not used	10
Time	Coded Word	2
Date	Coded Word	2
FAT	Word	2
File Size	Integer	4

Coded entries are read as required from look-up tables. The interesting thing to note about the directory entry is that it contains an entry which points to the FAT, the FAT is before the root directory on the disk and is the place that free sectors are stored. In other words it goes round in circles!

You will see that in the standard listing that there are four files with the.BAT extension. They are all less than 40 bytes long; it would be a great waste of space if MS-DOS put a file only 20 bytes long into a 2 Kb sector. The good news is that it doesn't, so let's have a look at the way that the FAT works.

Every disk contains not 1 but 2 copies of the FAT. However, the user only ever sees one of them as the other one is used by MS-DOS - we will come to this later. The FAT Table contains entries about the sectors based on the following table:

VALUE (HEX) (RANGE)	MEANING
0000	This Cluster is available
0002 - F1FE	Cluster in use by file (the number points to the

	next cluster used by the file)
0FF0 - 0FF6	**Reserved; not used**
0FF7	**Bad Cluster; do not use**
0FF8 - FFFF	**This is the last cluster in a file**

In MS-DOS Version 3.0 and greater, the FAT is a table of 2 byte entries with one entry corresponding to each cluster. Earlier versions of MS-DOS used 1.5 byte entries because the FAT table was a 12 bit number. Each entry, as listed above, tells MS-DOS whether the associated cluster is in use or not. It can also indicate where the next part of a multiple cluster file is stored and whether a cluster is bad. If a particular cluster is in use, the entry for that cluster either points to the next free cluster or the next entry for that file. In this case, then that cluster entry will take over the pointing function. A little simple maths will enable you to work out why there is a limitation of 32 Megabytes for a hard disk partition.

One unfortunate by-product of the way that MS-DOS works is that only one sector actually needs to be bad for the operating system to mark a whole cluster as being bad. However, when you look at the size of a modern hard disk then a few bad clusters is not too important.

A word of warning about bad sectors. When a disk drive is manufactured, it is tested for some time, usually 30 minutes or more. A very sophisticated device is used for the testing and if there are any faults on a drive then the machine will report them. These are then printed on a label which is glued to the drive casing - the Bad

Track Table. Most low level formatting programs will give you the opportunity to enter information from this table when a low-level format is being done. It is in your own interest to do so and the program will then mark these as bad. When you run FORMAT it will not then touch them - it is a false economy to try and squeeze every last bit of capacity out of a hard disk. Beware of the software which has recently appeared which is supposed to turn bad sectors in to good ones. They may enable a bad sector to store data for a short period of time but the long term reliability will be extremely suspect.

Anyway, enough of bad sectors - why are there 2 copies of the FAT? Quite simply, MS-DOS does not trust itself! Two copies are kept so that there is a reference point for utilities such as CHKDSK to use. If there was only one copy then CHKDSK would have to check every entry by actually going to it as it was found, and then doing a physical check. (It does not as it happens - it merely checks the FAT entries.) There would also have to be substantially more error checking at boot time if there was only one copy.

Formatting Utilities

One of the main differences, as far as hard disk drives is concerned, between an XT and an AT is that an XT disk controller is provided with its own low level format software. This is resident in a ROM or PROM and is accessed using DEBUG. Hard Disk Controllers for AT computers are not usually provided with this facility. The reason is probably because when the original AT specification was drawn up, a pre-formatted hard disk was included with the machine and this meant that the drive was fitted by the manufacturer. It was quite rare for the dealer or end user to ever have to do a low level format. With arrival of cheap AT's from the Far East and the desire to increase disk capacity, there also arose a need for software to perform a low level routine, but the very nature of the AT presented its own problems.

XT's are generally limited to a few capacities of drive. The MS-DOS limitation of 32 Mb partitions and the hard disk controller's limitation of two hard disks meant that as a general rule the maximum hard disk capacity of an XT is 65 Megabytes, i.e. two 32 Mb drives.

AT's are a completely different kettle of chips. There is not really a limit to the capability of the AT design to handle hard disks. It is theoretically possible to have seven 600 Mb hard disks running on one computer. This sort of storage capacity is way beyond most people's needs, not to mention their pocket! However, at the time of writing, a 300 megabyte drive can be had for about £1,000. This brings high capacity storage within the means of many more people than ever before. It was not very long ago that a high speed, 28 millisecond, 130 megabyte drive cost well over twice that.

So how is a hard disk formatted on an AT? Several companies offer software to do the job. We shall concentrate on two programs, mainly because they are the most common, and both have some nice features which make the job a lot simpler than other similar programs.

SpeedStor

If you need to low level format a drive for your particular AT it is worth checking before buying any formatting software to see if the MS-DOS utility disks have a small program called PREFOR. This is one of the best and fastest low level format programs but it does have a couple of limitations. Firstly, it will only format a drive that the BIOS in the computer can recognise - usually shown in the Drive Table which is accessed from the SETUP routine. Secondly, it cannot give you bigger partitions than 32 Mb when used with MS-DOS 3.n. (With Version 4.0 it will allow whatever MS-DOS will allow.) If you can't find PREFOR or you need large partitions, then you will need to use something else.

SpeedStor is a commercially available program and it costs around £80. The software comes on a disk, hence you must have at least one floppy drive available to run it, and it will work with the following controllers:

Western Digital WD1002S-WX1
Western Digital WD1002S-WX2
Adaptec 2002A
Adaptec 2010A
OMTI 5510-7
Data Technology DTC-5150BX
NDC Centran 5026
Western Digital WD1002-WA2
Western Digital WD1002-WAH
Western Digital WD1003-WA2
Western Digital WD1003-WAH
Data Technology DTC-5290
NDC Centran 5025

The first seven controllers are usually found on XT's while the remainder are AT specific.

SpeedStor is a disk specific utility and it will allow you to accommodate any standard hard disk, i.e. one built to conform the ST506/412 interface standard, of up to 195 Mb capacity with any IBM-compatible XT or AT which is running under MS-DOS. (Theoretically, the maximum sized MFM disk you can purchase is 127.5 Mb, while using RLL encoding increases the potential capacity to 195 Mb. If you want to use a greater capacity than this limit you need to use another controller type such as EDSI or, preferably, SCSI.) The program can also be used to identify and in some cases, correct disk errors. The program will permit you to overcome the 32 Mb disk size limit imposed by MS-DOS and have up to 8 separate partitions on one drive. The program suite is fully menu driven, making it easy to use and follow. Included in the suite are the following:

HardPrep - the program which low level formats the drive.

PartEd - the partition editor and formatter. Note that the primary partition, i.e. the one which is used to boot the hard disk, must be placed in the first 32 Mb of the disk. Thus you cannot make logical Drive-C non-bootable.

HarDrive - the device driver which allows the changes made with the other programs to be operable. Once this has been included in the CONFIG.SYS file, you will be presented with a message on boot up which details the logical drives and capacities of each.

The manual that accompanies the software is exceedingly good and it includes details of how to install a hard disk onto an XT and AT.

HardPrep

This is the program which performs the low level format on the drive. It also provides a range of diagnostic utilities which can be used for trouble shooting. To run the program simply enter HARDPREP, although you can include three command parameters which vary how the program operates;

/HELP does not activate the program but provides a list of the available command line options which can be used.

/NOCOLOR suppresses the normal colour display and presents everything in monochrome. Likely to be used only with corresponding monitor types.

/NOTYPE prevents the program from overwriting the ROM BIOS hard disk table.

Once the program is activated, a range of commands will be displayed along the top of the screen. The highlighter can be moved to one of these, and thereafter pressing Enter will activate the sub-command or bring up a secondary menu.

NextDrive will only appear if the system contains two physical drives. Its purpose is to allow you to move from one drive to another because HardPrep will only work with the drive you are currently logged on to, i.e. the one which is active.

ComposeBTT allows you to enter the defect tracks into the table, BTT being an acronym for Bad Track Table. These defects are found on the manufacturer's label and a note of them should be made before you install the drive unit into the system. The command contains a number of sub-options which are self-explanatory. Be warned that running the final sub-option, Media Analysis, will destroy any data already on the disk.

Diagnostics activates a sub-menu which contains the following commands:

Controller Test is used to run the controller internal self-test, useful if the disk does not appear to be functioning correctly, as the problem may be something as basic as an incorrectly applied cable.

Seek Test checks the seek ability of the disk using three types of test.

Read Random can be used, as many times as you wish, to test the entire disk non-destructively.

Write Random is similar to the above but it is destructive to any data already on the disk. It writes random data to selected sectors and then checks that this has been successful.

Initialise activates a sub-menu. This command need only be used when you are installing a new disk. It contains the following:

Interleave sets the interleave factor. By default, the program will use 3:1 on an AT disk and 6:1 on an XT.

Lock Tracks allows you to effectively discard any track that is bad so the controller does not try to use it.

Standard Init is the command which performs the low level format.

POD Fix is used for disks which do not match the type specified in the ROM disk type table.

Bounded Init performs the low level format only on specified cylinders and heads. This allows you to reformat a part of the disk, rather than the whole thing.

Type also activates a sub-menu, but the command is only available for use with AT's. The command allows you to harmonise disk drives of alternative types with those in the ROM BIOS. This is one of the main benefits that SpeedStor gives.

PartEd

PartEd is a partition editor that will allow you to create and format up to eight separate partitions on any hard disk. Each partition then becomes a distinct logical drive. One of the ways to speed up disk access with a drive using a standard controller is to create a primary 2 Mb partition which will contain the system files and the bulk of the MS-DOS commands plus a few batch files. The remainder of the disk can then be partitioned as normal and used as you wish. However, this only works effectively with disks using the ST506 interface; if you use EDSI or SCSI controller then you do not achieve any real benefit.

PartEd can be run as a command line with three parameters;

/HELP which displays the command options and does not activate the program.

/NOCOLOR activates the program in monochrome.

/DISPSECS displays the partitions in terms of sector numbers rather than by cylinder numbers.

Once run the program presents you with a menu driven screen in the same way as HardPrep, containing the available commands. The highlighter can be moved to one of these and thereafter pressing Enter will activate the sub-command or bring up a secondary menu. The commands available are:

Create which is used to define and build the partitions. You can have a total of eight partitions providing there is sufficient space to create them, i.e. you have not already used all the available capacity. Once a partition has been created you must high level format it using the Format command. You must not use FDISK or MS-DOS FORMAT when using SpeedStor - you can only use the commands that this program contains.

Next Drive allows you to log onto a different physical drive. Again, SpeedStor can only be used with the currently active drive.

Status is used to toggle the active partition. This must be bootable by MS-DOS created by PartEd or another operating system.

Type changes the system type used by the current partition.

Reorder allows you to change the logical drive assignments, e.g. you can move Drive-K to Drive-L and vice versa. The only partition that cannot be moved is C because it must be bootable by MS-DOS.

Delete removes a partition, e.g. so you can increase the size of an adjacent one. Any data that is contained in the partition being removed will be lost.

Format allows you to format the partitions which have been created using the above commands. You must use this command in place of the MS-DOS FORMAT.

SpeedStor is certainly useful and if you have purchased a disk with a higher capacity than the MS-DOS 32 Mb limit then it may be worth considering. However the program is not easy to find and it is quite expensive for what it does.

Disk Manager

Some computer and drive combinations are difficult to format using SpeedStor but as an alternative you can use OnTrack Disk Manager. The program is supplied with almost all Seagate and Miniscribe drives of 40 Mb and above. The versions supplied with these drives will only deal with the drives supplied by that manufacturer, e.g. Disk Manager supplied with a Seagate ST251-1 drive should only be used with Seagate drives because there are differences in the two versions of the program. However, there is also a general purpose version available which will do almost any drive but it is quite difficult to obtain.

The program has two modes of operation, either automatic or manual. I strongly recommend that like SpeedStor, it is only run in the Manual mode of operation. If you are using a colour monitor there is a colour option. The command line is: DM/M/C or DM/M where DM is the program name, /M tells it to operate in the manual mode and /C tells it to operate in colour mode. Make sure that the original program disk is properly inserted and type either of the above command lines. The first screen you will see looks like this:

DISK MANAGEMENT PROGRAM V3.62
Drive 1, 804 Cyls, 4 Hds, 26 Secs.
DISK MANAGER - MINISCRIBE
Version 3.62

PRODUCED FOR MINISCRIBE BY ONTRACK COMPUTER SYSTEMS

Many prompts provide help by pressing F1

MAIN MENU: HELP AVAILABLE BY PRESSING F1
(I)nitialization menu,
(P)artitioning menu,
(S)elect Drive,
(C)onfiguration menu,
(R)eturn to DOS
Select an option (R):

You will notice that along the top line it indicates that Drive 1 is 804 Cylinders, 4 Heads and 26 Sectors. This means that it has checked the CMOS memory in my computer and that holds the drive size information. There is also a copyright message and an indication that help is available. The main menu items are as follows:

(S)elect Drive. This is only required if you are formatting a second hard disk. If that is the case, select this option and tell it Drive 2 when prompted.

(C)onfiguration menu. This is the option to select if there is no message that says what size the drive is or you need to change the size or type of drive. If you select this option, this screen will appear:

DISK MANAGEMENT PROGRAM V3.62
Drive 1, 804 Cyls, 4 Hds, 26 Secs

DISK PARAMETERS (CYLINDERS by HEADS by SECTORS) are now STANDARD

Drive 1 is actually 804 by 4 by 26

CONFIGURATION MENU:
HELP AVAILABLE BY PRESSING F1

(S)tandard parameters,
(N)on-standard parameters,
(C)MOS configuration,
(W)rite configuration information,
(R)eturn to MAIN MENU

Select an option (R):

If you now select option N, the screen will show the drive table:

Enter MODEL CODE for drive 1
(1-23, or RETURN if standard):
Code / Model

01=3053	02=3085	03=3130	04=3180
05=3425	06=3438	07=3650	08=3675
09=6032	10=6053	11=6053	12=6074
13=6079	14=6085	15=6128	16=8051A
17=8425	18=8438	19=8450	20=8450XT
21=0920	22=9380	23=9780	

All the above numbers refer to Miniscribe drives in this case. If we were formatting a Miniscribe model 6032, that would be a type 9 and that is the number that should be entered. Once that number has been entered, press R or Esc to return to the main menu.

(I)nitialisation menu

This is the one that does the hard work of low level formatting the drive. First of all you must enter the bad track table as it is shown on the label which is fixed to the casing of the drive. For your own protection it is strongly recommended that you do enter the bad track locations. The screen for adding defects is shown below, and you can see that there is also the option to scan the disk surface for defects; - be warned that this option can destroy data, so take care if all you are intending to do is take a look at how Disk Manager works. Having entered the defect list, return to the previous menu and carry out the initialisation.

DISK MANAGEMENT PROGRAM V3.62
Drive 1, 804 Cyls, 4 Hds, 26 Secs

Cyl—Hd Cyl—Hd Cyl—Hd Cyl—Hd

CURRENT DEFECT LIST

DEFECT LIST MANAGEMENT MENU:
HELP AVAILABLE BY PRESSING F1
(G)et, (W)rite the defect-map FILE
(C)lear, (A)dd to, (D)elete from,
(L)ist the defect-list
(S)can disk for Defects,
(R)eturn to initialization menu

Select an option (R):

(P)artitioning

When it has performed the low level format, Disk Manager will require that the machine is rebooted. When the A-Prompt appears on the screen, you have two options if you are using MS-DOS 3.3 or better. With Version 3.2 or lower and a disk size of greater than 65 Mb you really have only the option of using Disk Manager's partition editor. If your drive is 65 Mb or less, we would strongly recommend the use of the FDISK program provided on your system disks. The reason for this is that FDISK will give you disk partitions without the need to resort to any form of trickery. Why use subterfuge when there is no need? With MS-DOS 3.3 or greater there is no need to use the partition editor in Disk Manager unless you want a very large second partition, and with DOS 4.01 that is catered for with its FDISK program.

If you do want to use Disk Manager's partition editor, there are several wrinkles to its use. Once again, use it in the manual mode; the way to invoke it is to enter DM/M/C or DM/M. When the opening menu appears, select (P) for partitioning and the following screen appears:

DISK MANAGEMENT PROGRAM V3.62
Drive 1,804 Cyls, 4 Hds, 26 Secs

CURRENT PARTITION TABLE
HELP AVAILABLE BY PRESSING F1

Does the above PARTITION TABLE require modification? (y/n):

This shows that there is no partition table on the drive. If you press Y, you will be asked Allocate by Megabyte (y/n). The easiest way is to answer in the affirmative which then brings up another menu:

PARTITIONING MENU:
HELP AVAILABLE BY PRESSING F1
(A)llocate,
(D)elete,
(S)elect boot,
(C)hange type, any partition
(N)ew partition table,

(R)eturn to preparation menu
Select an option (R):

Total DRIVE CAPACITY is 42 Megabytes.

Enter capacity, Megabytes, for partition 1 (default is 1 MB):

You will be forgiven for thinking that you now need to press A for allocate. Not so! What you need to do is write a (N)ew partition table, so enter N. Now enter the size of the first partition you require, under MS-DOS 3.n the maximum size of the first partition is 33 Mb, but you may split the drive in almost any way that you desire. For instance, you could have an MS-DOS bootable first partition of 1 Mb followed by a second partition of 31 Mb if you like, or any other combination so long as your first partition is a minimum of 1 Mb.

The alternative way is to allocate the partitions by telling Disk Manager to allocate a specific number of tracks to each partition. This can be done by answering N when asked if you wish to allocate by Megabyte and following the prompts.

Once you have finished allocating the partition table to your complete satisfaction use option (R) on the menu to return to MS-DOS. This will then ask you if you want to write the partition table to the disk. Answer Y and the partition table will be transferred to the drive.

There will then be displayed a message about how to get the drive to recognise the non-MS-DOS partitions. Our advice is to ignore these messages completely! We have rarely found that this part of the Disk Manager program to be all that successful. Over the years we have been using the program, we have devised our own way of doing it. By all means try the DM way, it's no great loss except for 10 or 15 minutes of your time if it doesn't work.

Our method is as follows. When Disk Manager has written the partition information to the disk and you exit to MS-DOS, it will reboot the computer. Use the MS-DOS FORMAT command and format Drive-C using the /S switch, i.e. place the system files on it. When formatting is completed, reboot from Drive-C to check that the format has worked and drive is actually bootable. Check to see if the other partitions are there but they won't be!

Now for the bit of magic to wake the other partitions up. Transfer the file DMDRVR.SYS from the Disk Manager Disk to the root directory of Drive-C. Now write the following CONFIG.SYS file in the root directory that drive, using **COPY CON CONFIG.SYS**.

DEVICE=DMDRVR.SYS
FILES=30
BUFFERS=30
Ctrl-Z Enter

If you need to add other device drivers, they can be included at this time or added later. It is important to place the DEVICE= DMDRVR.SYS at the beginning of the file. If you don't it is possible that other device drives will not be able to recognise any other partition that exists. Now reboot the computer, try to access the other partitions and hey presto, there they are.

The System Files

Whenever a computer is booted up, it carries out a series of actions - always in the same order. First it runs the POST program. The word is an acronym for Power On Self Test and it is simply a sequence of tests that the computer carries out to ensure that all the parts of it at working correctly. Normally the tests take less than a couple of seconds.

Once the POST is completed the first parts of the operating system is loaded - IO.SYS and MSDOS.SYS. These are the hidden parts of the operating system, the first controls the Input and Outputting of data to and from any source, while the second contains the bare bones of the operating system. In actuality the computer searches each of the default drives in turn to try and find the operating system files - which is why the floppy disk drive light comes on when you boot up. It searches though the drives until it finds the files it needs.

If the system cannot find either of these files, or if they have been damaged, the computer will hang up and you have a severe problem. The way out of the problem is to have a complete copy of the operating system on a floppy disk - any computer can always be booted from the floppy drive. Once it has been booted up you can try and correct the problem with the hard disk.

Next the machine loads COMMAND.COM. This is the main bulk of the operating system and it contains all the internal commands that MS-DOS possesses. Curiously enough you do not need to load this file - the system will work without it, but not correctly. Equally the three files must be from the same version of MS-DOS.

Once the basic operating system has been loaded, you can then apply your personal tailoring to it by creating, or copying, two additional files onto the hard disk; the CONFIG.SYS and AUTOEXEC.BAT. Both of these need to be in the root directory of the disk that contains the main operating system - you can place them elsewhere but let's not make things complicated. The first file is the one that allows you to configure the system to your personal tastes and preferences, hence its name. The second will automatically execute any programs or commands that it contains, including some counterparts of the files held in the CONFIG.SYS.

Both files are pure ASCII ones and they can be created by any word processor which is capable of generating such files, possibly called Nondocument files or ASCII files. However, as both files are normally very short, the quickest way to create them is to use **COPY CON [filename]**.

COPY is an internal MS-DOS command, i.e. part of the COMMAND.COM, and it allows you to do exactly what it says. In this case by including the word CON it means copy whatever is typed on the keyboard into the file named [filename]. You then type the commands you wish to include, each on a separate line. Once you have included everything you wish press **F6** or **Ctrl-Z** to terminate the input. The file will then be written to the current directory of the logical drive you are logged onto.

Note that for both of these system files and their contents to be activated you must reboot the machine by pressing **Ctrl-Alt-Del**.

CONFIG.SYS

Having loaded the basic operating system, the machine then searches the root directory of the primary disk to find the CONFIG.SYS file, loads it and then looks for an AUTOEXEC.BAT file. You don't have to have either of these. The system will work without them but not as you would expect it to. For instance, all computers are built as if they were to be run in the U.S.A. - because that is the largest market for them and that's where they were invented. Therefore if you want to use one in a different country you have to say so. This is one of the things that the CONFIG.SYS allows you to do. As an example here is a sample file:

```
COUNTRY=044
BUFFERS=30
FILES=30
DEVICE=C:\MS-DOS\ANSI.SYS
DEVICE=C:\MS-DOS\HIMEM.SYS
LASTDRIVE=M
```

The first line, COUNTRY, simply informs the operating system which national conventions to use for things like the Date, Time and Currency symbol. The three digit code is really the International Dialling Code of the country concerned. In the example above the 044 refers to the U.K. If you wanted to use the French conventions then you would use 033, in Spain the number is 034, etc. If you omit this line then the computer will continue to believe that it is being used in the U.S.A. so that, for example, pressing Shift-3 will produce a hash (#) instead of a Sterling sign (£).

The second line in the sample concerns the amount of memory that the system is to use as temporary storage for data. Whenever you ask to read or write something from or to the disk it is not transmitted immediately, instead it is held in a temporary store, the BUFFERS, until the computer can safely write to the disk without interruption. Because the machine is so fast you don't notice the delay, after all it is only milliseconds, but it is there none the less. The buffers command defines the amount of memory to be used. Each buffer uses 528 bytes of the RAM. Theoretically you can speed up the disk access by using a large number of buffers but if you make the value too large it has the opposite effect.

The types of program you are using have a bearing on the number of buffers you need to use. A word processor for example will need about 20; a flat bed database requires the same number; a relational database needs more; and a DTP program like PageMaker needs at least 30. In addition there are a couple of other considerations to be borne in mind. Firstly, any hard disk must have a minimum of 3 buffers assigned to it - it will not work properly with any less. Secondly, the amount of RAM you have available will have a bearing - the more memory you have, the more flexibility you can use with this statement.

The maximum number you can use is 99 but we have never heard of anyone, even on a network, using that many. The usual range is 20 to 40 and how many you use is entirely your own choice.

FILES simply refers to the number of disk files that the computer can have open at any one time.

Again this depends on the type of program you are using. DTP programs need more than most word processors - the number does not just refer to the data file you are using but to the entire program suite that might be necessary. For example when using WordStar 5.0 you open the main program file, the help file, the macros, the dictionaries, etc., plus any other data files you may have open while using the program. If you don't use this command or you specify too few files then the operating system has a fit and reports an error message. The number must be in the range 8 to 255 and each file will use 48 bytes of the RAM. Therefore in the file above you would lose 17,280 bytes, just under 17 Kb, to the Buffers and Files commands.

A DEVICE is any peripheral that is attached to your computer, e.g. a printer or a monitor. A device driver is the piece of software that controls the device. Certain devices are already known to the operating system and so they do not need to be specified, e.g. the keyboard, while others, such as a printer, will be identified only when a particular program uses them.

In addition to the hardware devices, there are also some special software ones. The first of these is mentioned above - ANSI.SYS. This is a driver that controls the monitor and keyboard, providing additional capabilities to the hardware drivers. These days it is not used much because the hardware has evolved to make it unnecessary but you may come across a program, especially a Shareware one, which must have the ANSI.SYS driver loaded in order for them to work properly.

The second device mentioned, HIMEM.SYS, is part of the Windows suite and it enables this program to work faster and more efficiently because it can use the extra RAM above the standard 640 Kb limit imposed by MS-DOS. This raises another important point about device drivers - each one must be on a separate line. Note also that the drivers are actually stored in a sub-directory - you should try to keep the root as uncluttered as possible, and by including the full path to the driver the operating system is able to find it. Other common device drivers are:

DISPLAY.SYS used in MS-DOS 3.30 and beyond.
DMDRVR.BIN is part of Disk Manager.
DRIVER.SYS supports external drives.
MOUSE.SYS is used with a mouse.
PRINTER.SYS also used in 3.30 and beyond.
RAMDRIVE.SYS creates a pseudo-drive in the RAM.

The final line in the sample file, LASTDRIVE, is only used in conjunction with large disk drives or if you have a large number of physical drives connected to your system - although this latter occurrence is rare. Because MS-DOS in all versions earlier than 4.0 cannot handle drives which have a capacity greater than 32 Mb, you have to partition a large drive into smaller chunks. (You can also partition a small drive of course, but it is rarely done.) Thus, if you had a 300 Mb drive you would end up with a minimum of 10 partitions and each would be treated, as far as the operating system is concerned, as a different logical drive.

MS-DOS assigns the letters of the alphabet to the partitions and/or drives as designators but makes no distinction between upper and lower case letters. They are shown as capitals on the screen only by convention. Thus you can have a maximum of 26 logical drives. By default the operating system can only handle five drives, A to E, and this is built into the system. The first two letters, A and B, are always reserved for floppy disk drives - even if there is only one fitted. You cannot use either of these to a hard disk partition, other than in exceptional circumstances. Thereafter, the remaining letters, C, D and E are used for the first three logical drives.

However, in the case of the large disk mentioned above, you have 12 drives as far as you are concerned but the operating system can only identify five of them, the first two being the floppies and the first three partitions being the other letters. In order to be able to use the other logical drives you must tell the operating system the maximum number of drives you intend to use by telling it what the last assigned letter will be, in this case M. But that's thirteen drives. Yes, because don't forget about the RAM Drive - that also needs a letter - and even though you might not intend using such a device it is as well to have a spare letter anyway. The drives are always named in a strict order. First are the two floppies, then come any other physical drives and their logical partitions, and finally the RAM Drive.

That concludes the explanation of the sample file. However, there are other commands that can be included in the CONFIG.SYS file. Here is a brief rundown of them.

BREAK

This command allows you to speed up the rate at which the operating system checks the keyboard for a manual interrupt. Many programs can be stopped in their tracks by pressing **Ctrl-C** or **Ctrl-Break**. Normally the keyboard is scanned by the operating system for either of these key sequences whenever a program is using the screen, keyboard, printer or auxiliary device. By including the line BREAK ON in the CONFIG.SYS the scan rate is increased so that the keyboard is also checked whenever a program accesses the disk or otherwise calls upon MS-DOS. In reality this command is no longer necessary because the keyboard scanning rate on modern computers is so fast the command has become redundant. (Note that most books would place this command in the AUTOEXEC.BAT but it works equally well here.)

FCBS

Another redundant command that is hardly ever used today. The letters are the abbreviation for File Control Blocks which was the method that MS-DOS Version 1.0 used to control files. Version 2.0 did not need the command because it handled the FCBS automatically. Equally Version 3.0 does the same but it restricts the number it uses. If you have a large number of files open you may get an error message saying '**FCB unavailable Abort, Retry, Ignore**'. This will only appear if you are using very old software - all modern software does not need to have extra FCBS assigned.

If you want to use the command, the correct statement is FCBS=X,Y. X refers to the maximum number of FCBS to use, Y restricts the automatic reuse of the FCBS by the operating system. By default the value for both X and Y is 4 but you can specify any number up to 255 for X or Y. Note however, that Y must always be equal to or less than X. Each FCBS used at X, over and above the default, will decrease the RAM by 40 bytes. If you are using the FILES command then there is really no need to use FCBS.

SHELL

This is very rarely used and then only in exceptional circumstances. The reason for its existence is that Microsoft assumed in the early days of MS-DOS that some programmers might build their own customised operating system in place of COMMAND.COM. The full expression of the command is:

SHELL = [drive] [path] [filename] [drive] [path] [/P] [/E:size]

The command and its effects vary from version to version, however it does have some similarities regardless of this. The first [drive][path] is optional and it simply informs the command where to find the alternative operating system. [Filename] is the name of the new command processor and you must include the extension if it is other than.COM, otherwise you can omit it. The second [drive][path] must be identical to the first and it simply informs MS-DOS how to get back once you have used the second processor. If you omit this then you are likely to find that the computer hangs up once you terminate the second processor. The parameter [/P] means Stay Permanent and it ensures that the main part of the MS-DOS operating system remains in memory. Again, if you omit this parameter then the computer will hang up on termination of the second command processor.

The final parameter [/E:size] determines the amount of RAM to be used for the new operating system environment and it operates slightly differently depending on which version of MS-DOS you are using. You must include the colon and not have any blank spaces. In version 3.1 it refers to 16-byte units and you can input a value in the range 11 to 62, i.e. totals of 176 to 992 bytes. (MS-DOS Version 3.1 and earlier use a 128 byte environment.) If you use an incorrect value then MS-DOS displays an error message then ignores the parameter completely and uses a default instead.

In versions 3.2 and 3.3 the size is specified in bytes, not blocks. The range allowed is 160, the default size, to 32,768 bytes and the value must be divisible by 16 - if it isn't then MS-DOS uses the next multiple of 16. For example, if you input /E:1876 then MS-DOS will automatically increase the value to 1888 or 16 times 118.

STACKS

Will be expressed in the CONFIG.SYS as STACKS=N,S where N is the Number of stacks and S is the Size in bytes. By default the number of stacks is 9 but this can be changed to any value in the range 8 to 64. The size is specified in bytes; by default it is 128 but can be anything from 32 to 512 - preferably in multiples of 16 but this is not essential.

A stack is an area of the RAM and it is used as a temporary storage area. As information is processed, the result is added to the bottom of the stack and then pushes up as more data is added. Once it gets to the top it is read off and used for further processing, the result of which can be added to the bottom of the stack again and so on. Each program has its own stack which can be anywhere in the computer memory. MS-DOS Version 3.1 could use any number of stacks, Versions 3.2 and 3.3 have a limit of nine stacks. When using some software, you can cause a fatal system crash by pressing a key while the program is working - it does not often happen - with the error message '**FATAL : Internal Stack Failure, System Halted**'. When, or rather if, this happens you must perform a cold reboot because the stack failure also disables the keyboard interrupts and so Ctrl-Alt-Del will not work. You can prevent the problem from occurring by increasing the number of stacks as above. However, it must be said that I have only ever encountered a stack failure twice. Personally, I would sooner know that a particular program causes the problem and then not use it!

AUTOEXEC.BAT

This file, again a pure ASCII one, is the final one to be loaded and run whenever you boot up the system. It does not have to be present - the machine works just as well without it - but as it performs a range of services for you it is well worth having. Generally speaking, the file will not be longer than 512 bytes and so it will occupy only a single sector. The filename tells you what it does, i.e. it AUTOmatically EXECutes the commands it contains. Again, we'll start with a sample and go on from there.

```
ECHO OFF
CLS
PATH=C:\MSDOS;C:\BAT;C:\UTILITY
PROMPT $P$G
C:\MS-DOS\KEYBUK
VERIFY ON
FR/SAVE
CLS
```

Whenever any command is activated by the operating system it always displays the name of the command as it does so. This process is called Echoing. MS-DOS provides a facility for turning the echo off - the first line in the sample file above. However, this itself is a command and so it will be echoed onto the monitor screen. Because my machine runs under MS-DOS 3.21, I cannot prevent this and so the second line is included to clear the screen after the first line is executed. If the machine was running under Version 3.3 or later then the first line could be preceded by the symbol @, i.e. @ECHO OFF, and this would turn off the echoing of the echo itself. The echo can be turned on again at any time by entering ECHO ON at the system prompt.

Whenever you input anything at the system prompt, MS-DOS assumes that it is the name of a file, i.e. a command. It then looks through all the files in the current directory to find a match. Should it find the file - it will then execute it. If the file does not exist there then the operating system returns an error message. If you were using a single directory, as on a floppy disk, then there would be no problem but the whole point of using a hard disk is to divide it into directories that contain associated files. Thus, if you wanted to run WordStar for example you would normally have to use CD\WS5 Enter WS Enter. The first half of the command changes to the relevant directory, while the second part runs the program. The more programs you have the more complex this becomes. Fortunately, MS-DOS provides an easier way in the form of the PATH command. Quite simply, this is a list of directories that will be searched to try and find a match for the keyboard input.

For instance, the third line above will search a directory named MSDOS - no prizes for guessing what this contains; then one called BAT, which holds all the batch files used to run other programs; then WS5, which contains WordStar 5; and finally another called UTILITY, which contains the majority of the utility programs I use. All this is in addition to searching the current drive and directory. In other words the total disk area that can be searched has been increased dramatically. Note that each directory is preceded by the drive designator letter and separated by a semi-colon. The drive letter is not essential but should be used especially if you have a number of logical drives, otherwise the operating system assumes that all the directories mentioned exist on every drive.

One major problem that occurs with the PATH command is that it can only be used to find program files, i.e. with an extension of.COM or.EXE, and batch files. Any program which then uses overlays, such as WordStar, cannot then find them because as far as the program is concerned, it is in one directory and the overlays are elsewhere. With programs that use overlays you are better off using a batch file that will log you into the correct directory before running the program rather than relying on the PATH.

PROMPT is an internal MS-DOS command, i.e. one that is part of the COMMAND.COM and hence can be run without having to have a separate program. Its purpose is to modify the appearance of the system prompt; the command mentioned will display the current drive and full directory path. There are a huge range of parameters that can be added to this command, which can be used singly or in combination to produce many different effects. Rather than explain them all in full, here is a brief description of each one.

B - produces a vertical bar, i.e. |
D - gives the full date, e.g. Thu 09-11-1989
E - produces an escape character
G - adds a greater than sign, i.e. >
H - causes a backspace, i.e. deletes the preceding character
L - produces a less than sign, i.e. <
N - causes the prompt to display the current drive designator.

P - displays the full path to the current directory
Q - yields an equals sign, i.e. =
T - displays the current time in full, e.g. 22:43:54.78
V - adds the MS-DOS version number.
_ - adds a character return - the prompt is on one line and you enter things on the next.
$ - a single dollar sign will remove the prompt completely and leave just the cursor. Two dollar signs produces a single sign, e.g. C:$
[message] - displays the contents of [message] - providing the ECHO is On.

To use any of the above simply add it to the end of the statement and precede each one with a dollar sign, e.g. PROMPT PD$B which would produce C:\Thu 09-11-89|. Using any other character, other than those above, will produce a blank space in the prompt.

The next line in the sample file is necessary if you want to use the computer keyboard as a British one. The line provides the complement of the COUNTRY command in the CONFIG.SYS. KEYBUK is a device driver and as such it must be available on the path so the operating system can find it. Because the file above includes the PATH before this statement the full path to the device driver could be left out, but it is much better to include it in full. In MS-DOS Version 3.30 the syntax of the command has been changed and now includes a space, e.g. KEYB UK, and you must also include additional information thus:

KEYB UK, [codepg], [drive] [path] KEYBOARD.SYS

The [codepg] refers to a new method of defining country codes and KEYBOARD.SYS is the new device driver. You can precede the command with a drive and path, as in the sample file, and the drive and path to the driver. The two letter country code can also be changed to reflect the coding you wish to use, e.g. FR for France, SP for Spain, etc. The command, in either form, is unnecessary if you want to use the computer as an American one because by default that is what the machine is. Note also that using either of the keyboard commands will use 2 Kb of the RAM.

VERIFY ON is used to force the operating system to check any file which is written to the disk. Normally any file sent to the disk is simply shunted to the controller which then places the file onto the disk - and it works exceedingly well. However disk drives do develop faults and by using this command you can get advance notice of such a failure. The command can be entered directly from the keyboard, i.e. at the system prompt, at any time but it is more usual to include it in the AUTOEXEC.BAT. If a fault does develop on the drive then this command will tell you so because the verification will not work, although it cannot tell you what the problem actually is. Should this happen then there is a high probability that the file you have just saved is corrupted or lost completely.

The penultimate line runs one of the Norton Utility programs. In this case it makes a record of where every file on the disk is stored so that they can be recovered if the disk is accidentally reformatted. The command produces a new file, FRECOVER.DAT, which is stored in the Root Directory of the disk.

The final line clears the screen again. This is necessary because the previous line produces messages on the screen which cannot be disabled through the ECHO OFF command.

The AUTOEXEC.BAT can include any MS-DOS command or other program name that you wish to run automatically on boot up. For instance, you could run a word processor by simply including its name and path at the end of the file. With front ends this is exactly what happens - the front end program name is included as the last line in the file so it will appear as soon as the full operating system is loaded and operable.

Directory Structure

A hard disk provides you with a large amount of storage space, even allowing for the 32 Mb partition limit that MS-DOS Version 3.2 and earlier demand. You could theoretically use the whole lot to store 33,554,432 characters - the equivalent of roughly five million words, or approximately 25 standard sized paperback books. No matter how you look at it that is a lot of space - in fact too much to store all in the same place.

That last sentence needs qualifying. The total amount of space is not too large (indeed under certain circumstances it is too small) it is the way that it is organised that is wrong. Using the analogy of the books, for a moment, you would not want to have 25 books all in a single volume. To start with it would be very unwieldy, heavy and awkward to manage. It is the same with a hard disk. A single 32 Mb partition is unwieldy - if you use it as a single data storage area. Ideally, what you need is some way of splitting the total area into smaller compartments - and MS-DOS provides it.

The 'trick' is to use directories and sub-directories. In actuality, everything is a sub-directory because it subtends off the Root Directory. But by convention, any such division within the Root is called a directory and any directory within one of these is a sub-directory. Building a directory structure is quite simple but it requires a bit of thought first and an explanation.

Any computer system can be considered as a Tree. The trunk represents the main hardware -

it is clearly visible and does not change. Attached to the trunk are branches, the various leads and wires, which in turn bear leaves, the devices such as a monitor, keyboard, printer, etc. The branches, but more especially the leaves, can change easily with extra ones being added or some being removed - on a yearly basis if you wish. As the computer system becomes more complex, so it acquires additional branches and leaves. All of the foregoing is the visible part of the computer system but it also contains an invisible element - the software which is on disk. The disk storage forms the roots of the computer tree. Each logical drive is represented by a main root and the directories and sub-directories thus become the rootlets. Individual files can be considered as the nodes on these roots.

The big difference between a real, live tree and our analogy is that you can chop and change the computer with ease - but you cannot easily modify a living tree.

Another way to consider a directory is as a filing cabinet. The Root directory of the logical drive is the equivalent of the entire cabinet. Any directory is analogous to a drawer and sub-directories then become the individual folders within the drawers. Files are thus the pieces of paper within the folders. The difference between a filing cabinet and a directory structure though, is that within the latter you can get at any other drawer, folder or piece of paper from within any other drawer or folder.

To create the basic structure you need first to know what programs, and their associated files, you want to have on your disk and a rough idea of how they are to be organised. Ideally, you want to keep the Root Directory as empty of files as possible it should contain only the system files, the CONFIG.SYS, and the AUTOEXEC.BAT - these could all be copy protected as a safeguard. Everything else should be in directories. One point that should be borne in mind is that a heavily layered directory structure is cumbersome and unwieldy. For preference, you should not have more than three layers, including the Root, although this may not be possible.

There are no hard and fast rules about a directory structure - simply some points to bear in mind.

1) A simple structure is easier to maintain and move around. If you make it complex and multi-layered then you will spend a lot of time moving through it to find the files you want.

2) Always place associated files together in the same directory. That way you can quickly find any given file instead of losing time looking for it. Remember what the directories are for - they make disk and file management easier.

3) Give directories simple, explanatory names. Many of today's software packages come complete with an installation routine, though some are better than others, and you will find that they tend to create directories that relate to the program. For instance WordStar Professional Release 5 uses WS5, PageMaker uses PM, Deluxe Paint II uses DPAINT2, and so on. You should adopt the same approach.

4) Plan the structure - don't just create it without forethought. A deliberate structure has a certain elegance and finesse to it, an indiscriminate one looks untidy and needlessly shoddy.

5) Always make a spare directory, one that can be used for copying files that you may want but are unsure about. If you have such a directory then you can copy the files to this, while you pick and choose which ones you actually want and then move them to their correct home. The unwanted ones can then be deleted quickly and easily. Never copy files into the Root Directory other than in exceptional circumstances.

Keeping these points in mind you can then begin to plan and finally create your directory structure.

Directory Commands

Because directories are special kinds of files they have to be manipulated with their own commands, of which there are three. The first, MKDIR or MD for short, an abbreviation for Make Directory, is used to create the directory using the syntax MD [drive]\[path]\[directory]. If the drive and path are omitted then the directory will be created as a sub-directory of the one you are currently logged onto. A directory name can be eleven characters long, eight as the main name and three as an extension, although it is common practise to not use more than eight - thus directories can be easily distinguished from filenames when listed using DIR/W. As with filenames you cannot use any of the reserved or forbidden characters or words.

It is possible to create directories at a distance, as it were, by including the full path. For example, if you had two logical drives and you wanted to create a directory on the second you could enter MD D:\[directory], while on any other logical drive and the directory would be created - note that you must include the backslash character after the drive letter. Equally you can create sub-directories in the same way by using MD D:\[directory]\[directory] - again each directory must be separated by a backslash.

The only error message you are likely to get using the command is 'Unable to create directory'. This will occur if you have tried to use any of the forbidden characters or words or if you are trying to create the same directory twice. You can only have one directory of any given name in any other directory. For example, suppose you had a directory called ALPHA in the Root. You cannot then have another directory of the same name at that level. However if you go down one level, even into ALPHA itself, and then input MD ALPHA you will have no problem.

To uncreate a directory you must use the command RMDIR, RD for short, the abbreviation for Remove Directory. If you were to use DEL [directory] then you would delete every file contained in that directory that was not Read-Only. This is a useful way of removing all the files but it does not remove the directory. The syntax for the command is RD [drive]\[path]\[directory]. As with MD, you can use the command at a distance to remove directories on other drives.

If, when you use the command, you get an error message saying Invalid path, not directory, or directory not empty it simply means what it says - one of the few examples where the error message is helpful! Either you have input the path incorrectly, misspelling it perhaps, or the directory name is wrong or the directory contains files. You cannot delete a directory that is not empty. You can check the first two possible causes by pressing F3 - this will display the last keyboard input again so you can check the spelling. If that is correct then the last cause is the only remaining culprit. Enter DEL [directory] to delete all the files and then try RD [directory] again. If it still will not work then you must move into the directory itself and physically check for the presence of files by using DIR. If there are no files visibly present then the most likely problem is that there are Hidden files. You can only get at these with a utility program, such as Norton or PC Tools.

To move around the directory structure you use the final special command, CHDIR or CD for short. This is an abbreviation for Change Directory and it allows you to do just that. The syntax is CD [path]\[directory] - note no drive specifier. You cannot change to another drive and directory in one operation. If while on C: you input CD D:\[directory] then nothing apparently happens. However if you then enter D: you will find that you are in the directory mentioned in the previous command. Normally though, you would change drive and then change directory.

The way you use the command syntax will also affect how it works.

1) CD [directory] allows you to move into a sub-directory of the current directory.

2) CD\[directory] allows you to move directly to another directory off the Root - you must obviously know the name of the target directory.

3) CD..\[directory] takes you back up one level and down to the named directory which is on the same level as the current directory. The two dots refer to the parent of the current directory. In certain circumstances they can refer to the Root but it is more normal to allude to the Root using the backslash. A single dot, which will be displayed when using the DIR command, signifies the current directory.

4) CD\ will take you directly back to the Root directory of the current drive.

5) CD.. simply takes you back up one level, i.e. to the parent of the current directory.

Chapter 6
CD-ROM

Overview

CD-ROM is one of the best kept secrets in the computer industry - everyone has heard of it but no-one seems to know what it is, what it does or where to get it. Yet the information is there, (however you have to dig hard and long to find it,) and there are over 250,000 users worldwide - although it has to be said that CD-ROM is used much more in the USA and continental Europe than it is Britain. Sweden and Switzerland in particular are heavy users of the medium. To put this figure into perspective, Microsoft Windows, in all its forms, has about the same number of users worldwide. In the UK. alone there are some 12,000 installed CD-ROM drive units. CD-ROM is available for both the PC and the Mac but there are many more PC applications than for its Apple rival; the ratio is about 9:1. As with all new technology there are a number of myths about CD-ROM which everyone knows, though they cannot say for sure how they know!

To start with, many people believe that CD-ROM is a storage medium which can be used to hold vast amounts of data. This is not true, or at least the first part isn't. CD-ROM is a publishing medium, not a storage device. It is on a par with books, microfiches or Read Only files rather than with magnetic disks. True, you can get a massive amount of data onto a disk - up to 550 Mb per disk - and that's a lot of information, the equivalent of some 400 books the size of this one! But it is not the same as standard magnetic computer storage. Come to that there are very few hard disks that have this kind of capacity. My new machine for instance has a mere 120 Mb of storage, in a device that can be very temperamental, cannot be moved easily, requires a special environment in which to work and weighs about 2.5 kgs.

A single CD-ROM on the other hand has nearly twice the capacity, is almost indestructible, can be transported with ease, can be exposed to air, water, heat, dust, etc. and it weighs less than an ounce. To give you an idea of the indestructibility of a CD-ROM: someone took his dog to the park and used a CD as a frisbee, throwing it and the dog catching and returning it. He, the human that is, then took the disk home, put it into the machine and it worked perfectly. Try doing that with a magnetic disk - but don't hold me responsible for the consequences!

CD-ROM is intended to be used for storing information and is unlikely to change in the near future. For example Boeing, the aircraft manufacturer, produce a huge number of different models and the parts list for each plane runs into thousands of items. At one time this listing came as a huge book and it took ages to find any specified item. Now the information is stored on CD-ROM, a couple of disks replace the entire library of parts volumes. The information does not change, after all an aeroplane does not change and it has a life expectancy of about 20 years, and so CD-ROM is the ideal medium to hold the information. The CD-ROM is more efficient and far cheaper than producing books - it costs around the same price to press a single CD-ROM as it does to produce a single book, thus making the CD-ROM 400 times cheaper, although it has to be said that the cost of collating the information and producing the master disk can be high. But once you have the master disk you can press as many duplicates as you need or want without any further hassle.

The next myth concerns price. Everyone knows that CD-ROM is very expensive, far too costly to be used by everyone. Again this is only partly true. The cost of an external drive unit is around £750 but then a 300 Mb hard disk is nearly twice that, so the price of the physical drive is actually cheaper. What is expensive are the disks themselves but even then you have to look at what you are getting. One of the most expensive disks is that produced by the Post Office, which lists every post code in the U.K. and the related addresses - all 23.5 million of them. It costs a mere £2,500, although that price includes regular updates. Now this sounds like a lot of money, and it has to be said that I wouldn't mind a bank balance of that sum, but you have to consider what you are getting. If it were sold as books it would cost around £6,000 for the same information plus a hefty amount for postage. But then this information is not intended to be used by everyone, it is aimed specifically at businesses, not at home users.

At the other end of the scale you can get a library of Shareware, containing over 500 separate programs, for a mere £99 or less. MirrorSoft have, at the time of writing, just brought out a new game - 'Defender of the Crown' - which includes graphics of film quality, a stereo sound track and spoken dialogue all for a mere £49.99, which is about twice what it would be on floppy disks, but you wouldn't get the same quality. Both of these are intended for home users and not for businesses - although they could be used by both. So in the U.K you can get CD-ROM's from £30 to £2,500 while in the USA you can get them from a little as $30 to $5,000. It depends on what the disks contain and where they are intended to be used.

One of the biggest problems with CD-ROM is the limited number of products that are available for it and thus the normal economies of scale don't, as yet, apply. Part of the problem is the sheer size of the medium, 550 Mb is a huge amount of storage, far more than you could realistically want except in very special circumstances. The result is that CD-ROM is not being taken up as a distribution medium, simply because there is no need for it. However if 'Defender of the Crown' takes off then you are likely to see a huge increase in the number of games which become available.

Many computer users denigrate games out of hand, often with very good reason, but it has to be said that games tend to be one of the driving forces in the industry. (One way to check the abilities of a computer is to run Flight Simulator on it. In the early days of the PC the machines were tested by playing Dungeons and Dragons on them! Personally I have to admit that I don't play computer games, except one 'Space M*A*X' and even that is a simulation involving building a space station and resource management not a true game.) Certainly if more games become available on CD-ROM then it will not be very long before more serious programs also become available. Just imagine the effects and capabilities of a CD-ROM used for training, one that was totally self-contained complete with video-quality graphics, sound and voice. It could revolutionise education - I wonder if anyone has suggested it to the Open University?

At the same time the cost of the drive units, while comparatively low, is still quite high - after all £750 represents a sizable fraction of the total cost of a computer system. Again though, to make any significant reduction in the cost of the units means that the economies of scale have to come into play. It is beginning to, but only slightly. For example you can buy a machine from Elonex complete with a CD-ROM drive and a number of Japanese computer manufacturers are beginning to incorporate the drives into their systems. (Rumour has it that one of the largest computer companies in the world is shortly to begin production of CD-ROM drives on a very large scale.)

The final myth, at least as far as we are going to cover them here, concerns the non-availability of CD-ROM disks - everyone knows that there are very few titles available. As with the previous myths this contains a single grain of truth but on the whole it is not true. There are now more than 3,000 titles available worldwide, albeit many of them are specialist titles, and the number continues to grow daily. Equally the number of CD-ROM drive manufacturers continues to increase. Gazing into the crystal ball one can see that CD-ROM is poised on the threshold of taking off in a big way.

Latest News

Corel Systems in Canada has just (December 1991) released CorelDRAW on CD-ROM. The complete package contains an internal or external CD-ROM drive, CorelDRAW on CD-ROM, the controller and some other goodies. The whole thing will retail at about £895. Considering that CorelDRAW itself retails at £449 this is a phenomenal price. And if you are a registered user of CorelDRAW then the price is even lower! CD-ROM is definitely coming into its own.

Adobe, Corel, Lotus, Microsoft, and other major manufacturers are all committed to supporting CD-ROM and you can expect to see it more and more over the next twelve months.

Construction

CD-ROM is based on Optical Technology, that it to say it uses a laser beam to read the information from the disk and then transfer it via a controller to the host computer. Unlike a magnetic disk the CD-ROM does not use concentric circles, rather it uses a single spiral on only one side of the disk. But let's start at the beginning.

A CD-ROM disk is 120 mm in diameter, slightly smaller than a 5.25-inch floppy disk, and it is about 1.2 mm thick or about the same thickness as the floppy disk in its sleeve. The disk is usually made of plastic, generally polycarbonate - the stuff they make bullet proof 'glass' from, which is coated with Aluminium and then a further protective layer of lacquer which is also 1.2 mm thick. The spiral on the disk contains tiny pits which are 0.12 micromillimetres deep and 0.6 micromillimetres wide - in other words you would need nearly two million of them to make a track 1 mm wide. The spiral is laid down so that you have a comparative figure of 16,000 TPI, as against 96 for a floppy disk or a few hundred for a hard disk. If you were to undo the spiral track and lay it out in a straight line you would find that it is nearly 3 MILES long and it contains nearly 2 BILLION pits.

The information on the disk has to be specially prepared, a process known as Mastering. Basically it involves transferring the original information, from magnetic tape, through a high quality laser onto a photogravure clean disk to create the pits and lands, the areas between the pits. The disk is then developed, rather like a photograph, and the result is a master disk. This disk is then used as a form from which all the distribution disks are pressed, usually by injection moulding. The resulting disk is the one you buy. It doesn't matter, by the way, whether you are talking about Compact Discs as used by the music industry or CD-ROM's used by the computer industry - the process is roughly the same.

In order to read the information on the disk you need a laser, generally a gallium arsenide one because it has a low wavelength and can be focused very accurately. The beam is focused down, through a lens, to a spot which is a mere 1 micromillimetre in diameter - which is just within the actual wavelength of the light itself. The light passes through the protective layer and 'reads' the reflections from the pits. The light hitting the pits is scattered much more, relatively speaking, than that which hits the lands. This signal is what represents the information stored on the disk. The reflected light passes into a photo detector which creates an electrical current that is directly proportional to the light intensity.

Within the drive unit there is no physical contact between the disk and the laser head, in fact the gap can be several millimetres, and so there is no possibility of the head ever hitting the disk. This allows for a CD-ROM disk to be slightly warped when it goes into the drive but it can still be read. Equally the protective coating means that no dirt or dust can get at the disk and the laser beam simply goes straight through any surface imperfection. No-one is yet sure how long CD-ROM disks will actually last, they haven't been around for long enough to tell yet, but in special tests they have been able to arrive at a figure of between 20 and 30 years as a safe life expectancy. That's the equivalent of some 5 to 10 computer generations, based on the current life span of PC's!

A single CD-ROM disk can hold an enormous amount of data as previously mentioned. Any single element of that information can be found within less than 1 second. CD-ROM is a random access medium, and the drive unit can be incorporated into a portable computer so you can take it anywhere in the world. CD-ROM is as significant in terms of data transmission as the original radio signal sent by Marconi, or the invention of the telephone by Bell, or the creation of a written language by the Sumerians and it is just as momentous.

However, to access this vast store of information you need special software and extensions to the MS-DOS operating system. A CD-ROM is treated as a single logical unit, it does not have to be partitioned into 32 Mb chunks thankfully, and that is what the extensions are for. When you purchase a CD-ROM drive you get the extension software with it and it is included in the price. Equally the software to access the information on the CD-ROM itself can be included, although some disks use the software that is part of the disk itself. Once loaded into the computer it can be used to extract the information quickly and efficiently, much faster than using a book for example, and you can generally customise it to your own environment.

One major point about CD-ROM is its compatibility. Any CD-ROM drive is compatible with any other, regardless of the machine it is used on. Thus you can, theoretically, use the same disk on a PC, Mac, DEC, HP, Sun, etc. Unfortunately the retrieval software tends to be machine specific and so this can defeat the object of the exercise. One other thing - a CD-ROM drive with audio output can also play CD Music discs, although you do need a special utility program to do so!

Fitting a CD-ROM

CD-ROM drives come in two forms, external and internal. The latter is no larger than a hard disk drive and it fits into a vacant slot in the carrier. To connect it, you simply attach the ribbon cables and power lines and secure it with the holding screws in exactly the same way as you would a disk drive, install the controller and software and away you go!

To use the external device you still need to open the computer casing, to insert the controller card, but then everything else is external. The device is supplied with the necessary cables and controller and it is strong enough so that you can place it on top of the system box and then put the monitor on top of that.

In both cases you can daisy chain a number of drives together, usually up to four, and so increase the amount of information you can access to a staggering 2.15 Gigabytes - all off one controller card. Price wise the internal drive will cost about £395 for a Hitachi CDR 3500, and the external one about £100 more for a Hitachi CDR 1503S. In fact the prices have just been reduced for the third time in less than a year. As more and more people use CD-ROM the prices will continue to fall.

Chapter 7
Data Organisation

Binary Notation

Whenever you use a program you make use of files, whether they are program files or the data that the program will use. As far as the computer is concerned all files are a form of data. This can lead to minor confusion because the word 'data' is now being used in two different ways - to you it means one thing while to the computer it is apparently something else. In actual fact everything that is used, manipulated or otherwise employed on the machine is simply strings of binary digits, bits, regardless of how it appears.

A binary digit, which is the minimalist expression of anything on or within the computer, is either a 0 or a 1 and by itself it is meaningless. However, when the bits are grouped together into strings or 'words' of 8 digits then they become useful - such a word is called a byte and this is the normal minimum quantity of data that the computer will deal with. A byte is the minimum amount of space that any individual character can be expressed in. Thus the English word DISK contains four bytes, this entire paragraph contains 635 bytes - a blank space is also a character, while the whole chapter contains kilobytes.

By convention, all computers make use of a system of encoding characters known as the ASCII Character Set. This was defined and agreed upon in the early days of computing, before the advent of the original PC in fact, and it provides for a maximum of 128 characters. The reason for the upper limit is because of the way in which the bytes of bits were organised and the way in which binary notation works.

Binary consists of a string of 0's or 1's, each digit having a positional value - in the same way as Denary does. For instance when you write the conventional number 236 the digits have a position value that corresponds with how far to the left the digits are. Thus, the above number means 2 Hundreds, 3 Tens and 6 Units. This is the system that we all learn at school and it is not as inherent as many people think. Watch a young child, say under four years of age, use numbers and you will find that they have little idea of the positional values, but by the time they are six or seven every child has learned what the positions of the digits means. In fact they learn it so well that they no longer think about it.

By the same token, children used to learn to count using other bases. (A base is simply the maximum number of digits that a counting system possesses, i.e. Binary contains 2, Denary contains 10 and Hexadecimal contains 16.) In the days before decimalisation everyone in the U.K. population used five different bases as a matter of course.

1) Base 10 used for 'normal' counting. We still use this today as it is the basis of all decimalisation.

2) Bases 12 and 20 for handling money. The former for counting Pennies, i.e. 12 Pence to the Shilling, and the latter for counting Shillings, i.e. 20 Shillings to the Pound.

3) Base 16 and 14 for dealing with weights. There are 16 Ounces in a Pound and 14 Pounds in a Stone.

As we were learning our numbers at school we automatically assimilated these additional bases until they became as inherent as Base 10 is today. One side effect of this is that children of those days had a better understanding of numbers than they do today and they could switch between the different bases without having to think about it, whereas today's children in general have a great deal of trouble comprehending anything other than the 'natural' Base 10.

Anyway, back to Binary. Each digit within a byte has a positional value that is exactly double the value of the digit to the right of it thus:

1 1 1 1 1 1 1 1
Binary
128 64 32 16 8 4 2 1
Denary

If the value is to be noted, and hence counted into the total, then the digit is given the notation 1, while if it is to be ignored as a value it is given the notation 0 - again this is not a value but simply a positional expression. Thus the Denary number 236 can be written in Binary as 11101100. This Byte then means: (1*128) + (1*64) + (1*32) + 0 + (1*8) + (1*4) + 0 + 0 = 236.

Using 8 Bits to a Byte will allow a maximum Denary value of 255, i.e. 128 + 64 + 32 + 16 + 8 + 4 + 2 + 1 = 255.

Therefore you would expect that the ASCII character set would contain 255 separate characters, i.e. the maximum number, but this is not the case. The original ASCII set only contained 127 characters because they used 1 digit as a check digit and using a single binary for other purposes automatically halves the total value and then subtracts 1 from the result. The original ASCII set is as follows, discounting the first 31 characters as they perform special operations:

32	00100000	Space	33	00100001	!
34	00100010	“	35	00100011	#
36	00100100	$	37	00100101	%
38	00100110	&	39	00100111	‘
40	00101000	(	41	00101001	)
42	00101010	*	43	00101011	+
44	00101100	,	45	00101101	-
46	00101110	.	47	00101111	/
48	00110000	0	49	00110001	1
50	00110010	2	51	00110011	3
52	00110100	4	53	00110101	5
54	00110110	6	55	00110111	7
56	00111000	8	57	00111001	9
58	00111010	:	59	00111011	;
60	00111100	<	61	00111101	=
62	00111110	>	63	00111111	?
64	01000000	@	65	01000001	A
66	01000010	B	67	01000011	C
68	01000100	D	69	01000101	E
70	01000110	F	71	01000111	G
72	01001000	H	73	01001001	I
74	01001010	J	75	01001011	K
76	01001100	L	77	01001101	M

78	01001110	N	79	01001111	O
80	01010000	P	81	01010001	Q
82	01010010	R	83	01010011	S
84	01010100	T	85	01010101	U
86	01010110	V	87	01010111	W
88	01011000	X	89	01011001	Y
90	01011010	Z	91	01011011	[
92	01011100	\	93	01011101	]
94	01011110	^	95	01011111	_
96	01100000	‘	97	01100001	a
98	01100010	b	99	01100011	c
100	01100100	d	101	01100101	e
102	01100110	f	103	01100111	g
104	01101000	h	105	01101001	i
106	01101010	j	107	01101011	k
108	01101100	l	109	01101101	m
110	01101110	n	111	01101111	o
112	01110000	p	113	01110001	q
114	01110010	r	115	01110011	s
116	01110100	t	117	01110101	u
118	01110110	v	119	01110111	w
120	01111000	x	121	01111001	y
122	01111010	z	123	01111011	{
124	01111100	|	125	01111101	}
126	01111110	~	127	01111111	

Using the ASCII set any of the standard characters can be rendered as a series of Bytes, e.g. ASCII itself written in binary is 01000001 01010011 01000011 01001001 01001001. The computer takes the input from the keyboard, which it reads as strings of Bytes and then converts it to standard Roman characters on the screen where you see it. But the important point is that the computer handles all the characters as binary, the expression of this as the normal characters you see is for your benefit, not the computer's.

One final point. Binary notation, while simple, is very wearing on the eyes - those strings of digits tend to blur into each other making them difficult to read. Therefore it is not normally used by people, instead they use another notation called Hexadecimal, i.e. Base 16, usually abbreviated to Hex. If you are used to working with Pounds and Ounces this should present no great difficulties except that it uses additional characters so that it contains 16 digits. The Denary digits 0 to 9 are used as normal but the following letters are appended to the series to provide the additional digits required;

A = 10	B = 11	C = 12
D = 13	E = 14	F = 15

It is customary to write a Hexadecimal number as H12, i.e. preceded by an upper case H, or 12h, so as to denote that you are dealing with this Base. The advantage of using Hexadecimal is that the strings of binary digits are replaced by short, two or three digit values, making them much easier to handle. For example, the Denary number 236 is 11101100 when written in Binary and ECh when written as Hexadecimal. But remember that Hex is an aid to humans - the computer continues to use Binary.

Data Storage

Even though the individual characters that make up any file are stored as Bytes, there is slightly more to it than that. When a file is written to the disk the computer does not write the characters individually or at least not as individual entities. On any computer, whether it be a PC, XT or AT, there is a minimum amount of storage capacity that the machine will use at any time known as the CLUSTER size. The Cluster is a block of Sectors, which in turn are divisions of the Tracks on the relevant disk and the size of the Cluster depends on the type of disk being used. Any file that is then stored on the disk will occupy a Cluster as an absolute minimum.

Disk Type	Sector	Cluster	Total
5.25" 360 Kb	512 Bytes	2 Sectors	1024
3.50" 720 Kb	512 Bytes	2 Sectors	1024
5.25" 1.20 Mb	512 Bytes	1 Sector	512
3.50" 1.44 Mb	512 Bytes	1 Sector	512
MFM Disk	512 Bytes	4 Sectors	2048
RLL Disk	1024 Bytes	4 Sectors	4096

Thus, if you were to save the save file containing 240 characters onto each of these disk types you would be using a different amount of space each time. On both the low density floppies the file occupies 1 Kb, i.e. 1024 Bytes, while on the higher density disk it only occupies half that amount. (This sounds like an anachronism but it is due to the fact that high density disks make more efficient use of their space than do low density ones - indeed this is one of the primary reasons for using them.)

But on the MFM disk the file uses 2 Kb and on the RLL disk it occupies 4 Kb of space. With a small file, i.e. one that is smaller than the Cluster size, this does not matter too much. It is when the file exceeds the Cluster size by a single character or Byte that you suddenly begin losing vast amounts of space needlessly.

For example, take a file that is 1025 Bytes, which is stored on a low density floppy disk. This will require 2 Clusters in order to store it, but in the second Cluster only a single byte is being used. Therefore on the disk there is 49.95% of the Cluster space being wasted.

Using a high density floppy and a file of 513 Bytes there is 49.90% wastage. Slightly less but still a lot.

On a MFM disk and a file of 2049 Bytes the wastage is 49.97%, and on an RLL disk using a 4097 Byte file the loss is even worse at 49.99%

If you have a number of files that all fall into this wasteful category you will soon end up bouncing off your disk capacity limit when in actual fact more that 40% of the disk is unused. Therefore it is in your interest to be aware of the Cluster size your disk is using and to try and keep your files of such a size that they make the best use of the Clusters.

Disk Terms

There are a number of other points and terms that you need to be aware of when using a hard disk. They also apply to floppies, but as these are low capacity when compared to a hard disk, and also inherently slower, they are of less concern.

Access Time

The Access Time is a measure of how fast the computer can access a given file and it is a composite figure based on the Seek Time and the Average Latency. However, there comes a point when the access time is effectively pointless and that is when the file is being accessed faster than you, i.e. the human operator, can handle. This is one of the great fallacies about computers - they might be becoming faster and faster but the human operators are not, in fact the statistics tend to show the exact opposite, and therefore radical improvements in the speed of operation are redundant. Where the seek time does become important is when you are using software that automatically loads a number of files itself. The speed of the program loading can be improved by using faster access time disks.

The access time is usually expressed as the Average Access Time. This is a measure of the period required for the Read/Write Heads to move from their present position to the beginning of a another file that you want to read. The average is normally the amount of time that it takes the heads to move across one third of the tracks. However, by using a good compression program, such as Speed Disk from Norton or Compress from PC Tools Deluxe, you can actually access the files faster than the expressed time.

Average Latency

Quite simply this is the time taken for the disk to complete half of one revolution and it is a measure of the time required for the correct sector to move beneath the Read/Write Heads. With most hard disks spinning at 3600 RPM, i.e. performing a single revolution every 16.67 milliseconds, the average latency is therefore 8.3 ms. The latency is normally measured as part of the access time and is rarely mentioned otherwise - after all, every hard disk spins at approximately the same speed and therefore the latency does not change very much from disk to disk.

Seek Time

This is simply the time required for the Read/Write Heads to move to the track of a particular platter that holds the file you have asked for. Note that is not the time taken to load the file but the period required to find the file, or rather the beginning of it. Seek Time is measured in milliseconds, abbreviated to ms, and with the majority of disks the time will fall in the range 18 to 100 ms. Obviously the faster the seek time the quicker you can use the file.

Track to Track Rate

The Track to Track seek time is a measure of how fast the Read/Write Heads can move from one track to another adjacent one. Generally it is included as part of the Access Time. Using an MFM disk will give a Track to Track rate of roughly 10 to 12 milliseconds, whilst RLL drives are slightly faster. IDE drives will give better times as will ESDI and SCSI drives.

Transfer Rate

This is probably the most important figure you can ascertain about the disk - it is a measure of how fast the data can actually be read from the disk and moved into the computer's memory for processing. The Transfer rate is measured in Bits per Second. Generally speaking the rate is quoted in disk drive adverts but not on the disk itself. There is no simple way to check the transfer rate directly from MS-DOS - but if you use the SpinRite utility program it will give you a highly accurate reading of this.

The average Transfer rate for most AT disks is around 5 Mb per second, regardless of whether they are MFM or RLL encoded. A more modern interface, such as EDSI, can double or even triple this figure. However, there is very little point in using an ultra-fast interface if the computer itself is running at a slow speed, i.e. less that 12 MHz.

Interleave Factor

The final ingredient that has a bearing on the speed with which the computer, via the controller, can access the data, is the Interleave Factor. When data is written to the disk it is 'laid down' in the cluster blocks, i.e. within sectors, but because the disk is spinning at a fast rate, usually 3,600 RPM, the disk surface moves under the Read/Write Heads rather quickly. The result is that the file being written is not necessarily placed into consecutive sectors - instead the Interleave Factor comes into play. This is usually expressed as a ratio, e.g. 1:1 or 3:1, which informs you which sectors are written to and which are skipped, before the next write operation.

Thus an Interleave Factor of 3:1 means the controller writes to 1 sector then misses the next two before writing to the fourth, misses 5 and 6 and then writes to the seventh and so on. What really happens is that the sectors are not numbered consecutively, instead they are numbered so that the serial order reflects the Interleave Factor.

The Interleave Factor has an enormous bearing on the speed with which data can be throughput but this must work in conjunction with the computer itself. With the majority of AT's an Interleave factor of 2:1 is the norm, although the number of machines with 1:1 Factors is increasing constantly - especially on IDE drives. The Interleave Factor is normally handled directly by the MS-DOS Low Level Format command, However, if you have a copy of SpinRite, you can use this to maximise the disk's potential and change the factor if necessary.

Disk Commands

MS-DOS comes complete with a range of commands that are specifically concerned with handling disk drives. After all, the phrase is an acronym for Disk Operating System. This book is not intended to cover them in depth; there are a large number of good MS-DOS books available and every computer comes complete with a MS-DOS manual. Instead what follows is a brief look at each specific command - in alphabetical order.

ASSIGN

Every computer automatically comes with two logical drives, A and B, even though there may be only 1 drive physically present. By default these two letters are always reserved for the floppy disks. A logical drive is one that is apparently present, while a physical drive is the material piece of hardware. Thus you can use a single floppy drive as either A or B, although you will be prompted to place a disk in either as you switch between them. Normally, However, you would stick to using A. If you have a second physical floppy installed then this becomes B, automatically, and you cannot use the A-Drive as either. So far so good, but what happens when you are using software that demands you have the program in one drive and the data stored on another? Such an occurrence is rare today but at one time it was common practise and a number of older software programs will not function correctly if you do not do so. There are two ways to get round the problem.

1) Get rid of the old software and replace it with a more modern package. Unfortunately this is not as simple as it first sounds, especially if you have a large number of files generated by the old program which then have to be converted. However, in the long run this is actually the best answer. Modern software makes better use of the computer's method of operation, it is faster, more efficient and has a lot more features.

2) Cheat! MS-DOS comes complete with a special external command called ASSIGN, the purpose of which is to force the computer to treat one logical drive as another and ignore the presence of the physical drive in the process. To activate the command use the line ASSIGN [drive 1]=[drive 2] where Drive 1 is the one which you wish not to use. Because the command is an external one it must be either physically present on the drive you are using or available on the PATH. Thereafter, whenever the program requests access to Drive 1 the computer automatically routes it to Drive 2 without the software being any the wiser.

Using the command will affect any and all subsequent access to Drive 1, effectively masking the presence of the drive - so much so that it might as well not be there. You can deactivate the command at any time by entering the command name without any parameters at the system prompt, i.e. ASSIGN, and all drives will return to their original status.

ATTRIB

Any file which is stored on a disk, whether floppy or hard, must have a number of attributes to it. The first is the filename, a string of up to eight characters, which is normally assigned by you. Next is the file extension, containing up to three characters. This may be created by the user or with some programs it is automatically created for you. The next two attributes are the Date and Time stamps. These are automatically emplaced by the computer whenever the file is saved to the disk. Whenever you use the DIR command, these attributes, along with the actual number of characters the file contains, are what you see, although if you use DIR/W then you will only be able to see the filename and extension.

However, in addition to these obvious ones there are four other attributes which a file can possess and two of them can be changed by you. To see the attributes use the command ATTRIB *.*. This will display a list of the files in the current directory, very similar to the one you get using DIR, except that the filenames will be preceded by letters and their path location, e.g. A R C:\MS-DOS\ATTRIB.EXE

The first letter refers to the Archive bit. (These attributes are also called bits because they are turned on or off by altering a single binary digit.) Whenever a file is created or resaved this attribute is turned on and thus the letter A appears when you use this command. The archive bit is used to designate that the file is new and thus it will be duplicated by a backup program the next time one is used.

Once the file has been backed up the archive bit is spontaneously turned off until the next time the file is modified or resaved. In addition you can turn the bit on and off yourself by entering ATTRIB +A [filename] or ATTRIB -A [filename]. A plus sign turns the bit on while a minus sign turns it off. You can also use the command with the wildcard characters to change the bits on a number of files at the same time.

The second letter, R, refers to the Read Only bit. Any file which is Read Only cannot be changed, nor can it be erased. Some programs will create files that have the bit set, e.g. Norton Format Recover, but generally the bit is not used by software. Again, as with the Archive bit above, you can turn this one on and off yourself by substituting R for A. You can also combine the two attributes into one command, e.g. ATTRIB -A +R *.* which turns the Archive bit off while making the files immutable.

There are two additional attributes, System and Hidden, which can be applied to files but these can only be changed by using a special utility such as Norton Utilities or PC Tools. Every computer system has at least two Hidden, System files - IO.SYS and MSDOS.SYS, and these usually have all four bits on as extra protection.

BACKUP

This is exactly what it says, a program that will create backup copies of your files onto pre-formatted diskettes. It will backup all those files, in the current directory, that have their Archive bit set On. If you have changed this, using either the ATTRIB command or a utility, then those files will be ignored. Once a file has been backed up MS-DOS will automatically change the Archive attribute to Off so that it knows which files have been backed up for future reference.

One problem with this command is that different versions of it, e.g. those from MS-DOS 3.2? and MS-DOS 3.3?, are not compatible - in other words you cannot make a backup with Version 3.21 and then restore it with Version 3.30, or vice versa. Another complication is that the disks onto which the backup copies are made must be formatted before use. The final obstacle is that you cannot ask it to deal with specific files: it will copy every file in the source directory or drive.

You can add a wide range of parameters to the command, which has the format **BACKUP [drive] [path] [drive] [parameters]**, to produce a range of different conditions.

/A causes the command to add the new backups to the old ones already on a disk. In the normal course of events one backup will automatically delete the previous one but with this parameter you can prevent that.

/S tells the command to backup the sub-directories as well as the files thus you can use the command to backup your entire hard disk - but have lots of floppy disks ready if you choose to do this.

/M forces the command to backup only those files which have changed since the last backup was made.

/D: [date] tells the computer to only backup those files that were last modified on or after the date specified. Thus you can use the command to be selective about the files that are copied.

/P means pack as many files as possible onto each disk, i.e. fill the disk even if this means fragmenting the files.

/T: [time] allows you to backup only those files that have been modified or created on or after the specified time.

/L: [filename] this allows you to change the name of the default file that the command uses to store its information, i.e. normally called BACKUP.LOG.

You can use the command to make backup copies of your files either to floppies, which is the usual method, or to your hard disk. Backups are especially important if you have a hard disk machine as they provide you with protection against data loss in the event of a disk crash.

CHDIR

The acronym for CHange DIRectory, which can be further abbreviated to just CD, it allows you to move through the directory structure of the disk, accessing the various sub-directories as necessary. In addition, by entering the command without any parameter it will tell you the name of the sub-directory you are in - although if you use PROMPT PG in the AUTOEXEC.BAT this will not be necessary.

The full formula for the command is CD [path] [directory] but it is rarely used like that. The command can make use of two parameters, \ and.., which affect how you move through the directories. The former will always take you back to the root directory of the disk you are currently logged onto. In fact the backslash character is generally used to denote the root directory, whilst the two dots are used to take you up one level of the structure. For example, suppose you had a structure that contained the following directories;

```
C:\
   \ALPHA
         \ONE
         \TWO
   \BETA
         \BAKER
   \GAMMA
         \UNE
```

To move directly from the Root into Gamma you would enter CD GAMMA. Having performed an operation there to move back to the Root you would enter either CD\ or CD.. - because in this case both target directories are the same, i.e. the Root is parent to Gamma.

If you wanted to move to TWO from the Root you would enter CD ALPHA\TWO. Once there, if you then wanted to go to ONE you could either enter CD\ALPHA\ONE, i.e. move back to the Root and then down the structure again to the target, or more simply CD..\ONE. This latter form will move you back to the parent of the current directory, i.e. ALPHA, and then straight down to ONE. Note that you must separate each directory with a backslash character - but it is only when the backslash immediately follows the command that it refers to the Root.

To move into BAKER from the Root enter CD BETA\BAKER. If you then want to move into UNE you have to go back to the Root first by entering CD\GAMMA\UNE - but you do not have to specify every directory back to the Root along the way.

In actuality it does not matter which method you use - MS-DOS always goes back to the Root and then down through the structure to get to any target directory, but does it so fast you do not notice!

CHKDSK

Abbreviation for CHecK DiSK, this program will analyse your disks, either hard or floppy, and check the directories and files to make sure that they have been saved properly. Once the analysis is completed it will then display a report of the disk's statistics as well as the computer's memory, e.g. checking a 20 Mb hard disk might give a report like this;

21282816 bytes total disk space
57344 bytes in 6 hidden files
51200 bytes in 23 directories
11913216 bytes in 538 user files
2048 bytes in bad sectors
9259008 bytes available on disk
655360 bytes total memory
582800 bytes free

A bad sector is one that contains a physical error and thus it cannot be used for data storage. It is possible to extend the report if you wish by adding /V to the end of the command and so force it to list the name of every directory and file on the disk as the command encounters and checks them. Alternatively you can use the command to check on a single file by entering **CHKDSK [drive] [path] [filename]** in which case the computer will display a message if the file is non-contiguous - i.e. fragmented. You can use the wildcard characters with this command and so check a group of files. The command can also be used to fix Lost Chains, i.e. fragmented files, but it is easier to use the Norton Disk Doctor command instead.

COMP

One of the most important things that you will need to do when using the computer is make backup copies of your most important files, either by doing a straight duplication using the COPY command or by using BACKUP. However, a problem can then arise because you can end up with a large number of floppy disks that contain these copies and you do not know which is which. Granted that you can find out which is the later version of the file by using the time and date stamp - that is what they are for after all - but you might actually want to compare the files themselves. You can do this by reloading the files into the application that produced them in the first place, but that is long winded and there is a simpler way: use this command.

COMP allows you to compare any two files, byte by byte, and it then produces a report of any differences between them. In fact it only tells you about the first ten differences but if there are any more than that then the files are obviously radically different! To use the command just place the floppy disks in the drives and then enter **COMP A: [filename] B: [filename]**. If there are no differences then the computer will tell you that the 'Files compare OK' otherwise you will get a report detailing the differences.

You can also use the command on a single drive machine by entering **COMP A: [filename] A: [filename]**. If the files you want to check exist on different disks then you just have to swap them over when the computer prompts you to do so. The command can also be used to compare files on a hard disk, rather than on floppies, by using **COMP [drive] [path] [filename] [drive] [path] [filename]**.

COPY

This is the one command that you are likely to use more often than anything else - it is certainly one of the most versatile and beneficial ones that MS-DOS contains. The full structure for the command is **COPY [drive] [path] [filename] [drive] [path] [filename]** but it is rarely used like that. Instead it is more common to move into the source directory and then copy the required files to the target using **COPY [filename] [target]**.

Suppose you wanted to copy the files from BAKER to the Root. There are a number of ways to do so.

1) Whilst in the Root enter **COPY \BETA\BAKER*.***. Note that you do not have to specify the drive because you are staying on the same one - it is just the files that are being operated on. You must include the three backslashes, though. Note that the source is mentioned but not the target - because you are in the location where the files are to be copied to. The files will be copied and as each is dealt with its name will be displayed on the screen. (You can avoid this by appending >NUL to the command.)

2) Move into the Source directory, using **CD\BAKER\BETA**, and then enter **COPY [filename] C:**. Again you do not need to

specify a drive because you are simply copying files on the same unit. In this case you mention the Target but not the Source.

3) From anywhere on the disk you can enter **COPY C:\BAKER\BETA\ [filename] C:**. In this case you must provide both the Source and Target designations. In fact, using the command in full like this you can even use it across logical drives, e.g. use the command as stated whilst you are logged onto another drive.

The Wildcard characters add a further degree of power and ability to the command. You can also use the command to produce a printed copy of a file by entering **COPY [filename] PRN**.

DEL

This command allows you to DELete files from anywhere on your disks, providing that the files have not been protected by having their attributes changed. The command is very powerful, especially when used in conjunction with the Wildcard characters, and for this reason you should take care when using it, otherwise you are liable to find that you have deleted a whole range of files that you wanted. In use the format for this command is **DEL [drive] [path] [filename]** and it is used in the same way as the COPY command.

DIR

This command allows you to list all the files contained within the current directory. By entering DIR, short for DIRectory listing, you will be presented with a schedule of all the non-hidden files in the current directory of the current disk. Along with the name of the files you will also be shown their sizes and the time and date when the files were created, e.g. COMMAND COM 25308 1-12-88 12:00p. Should you have a large number of files the display will scroll up before you have a chance to read to the first ones, especially when using a 286 or 386 based machine. There are three ways in which you can stop this.

1) Use **Ctrl-S** to stop the scrolling effect at any time. Press both keys together and the display will freeze. Pressing any other key will start the display again. This works well, once you become used to hitting the right keys, but there is a better way.

2) Enter **DIR/P** and the computer will display the listing in chunks of 20 lines at a time and the display displays a message saying **Press any key...** You then have time to examine the filenames. Pressing any key presents the next 20 files and so on.

3) If you are not concerned with the size, date and time, you could enter **DIR/W**. This will give you the directory listing in five columns across the width of the screen but exclude the superfluous detail.

You can combine the pause and width options if you have a very large number of files by entering **DIR/P/W**. This will give you a five column display that pauses every twenty lines.

If you want to know if a particular file is present you can enter the command in the form **DIR [filename]**. If the file is present it will be listed, otherwise you get a message saying 'File not found'. You can also use wildcards here as with the DEL command. To use the command across disks and directories use the command in full, **DIR [drive] [path] [filename] [parameter]**.

DRIVER.SYS

A computer comes complete with a disk drive or two already installed and ready to work. However, the creators of MS-DOS recognised that there might come a time when a user would want to install additional drives - possibly even externally - and this file is the result. Note that this is a device driver, not a command.

It works in the same way as ANSI.SYS or RAMDRIVE.SYS in that it allows you to introduce additional elements to your computer system. To use the command you need to include a line DEVICE= DRIVER.SYS in the CONFIG.SYS file, and you must have already set a sufficient number of disk drives to allow for it. By default MS-DOS can handle up to five drives, labelled A to E, but if you have already used up these letters with your internal drives then you must increase the drives allowable by using, for example, LASTDRIVE=H in the CONFIG.SYS before you use the line that installs the external drive. In actuality it is unlikely, in the normal course of events, that you will want to install an external drive, but the provision is there if you need it.

FDISK

This command provides you with four options, all of which are available from a short menu. Warning: Be very careful using this command or you may find yourself losing all the data on your hard disk!

1) Create DOS partition - A partition is, basically, an area of the hard disk that MS-DOS recognises as an individual disk drive. For instance if you have a 40 Mb hard disk and you are using MS-DOS 3.20 then the maximum size of disk permitted is 32 Mb. Thus you would have to partition the disk into two and these would then become Drive-C and Drive-D - the size of the partitions within the 32 Mb limit is irrelevant but it helps if you make them as large as possible. Once you select this option you will then have to input the size for the partition and MS-DOS will do the rest. If the disk is already partitioned then the operating system will tell you so and the entire process will terminate.

2) Change Active partition - Allows you to modify partitions already in existence. However, don't do this if you have data on the disk or you will definitely lose it. One of the main reasons for changing the partitions is that you can have different operating systems on each one, e.g. MS-DOS on one and UNIX

on another. But generally speaking once the partitions have been created you will not normally want to adjust them.

3) Delete DOS partition - Does exactly what it says, and wipes out all the data in the partition in the process because you will then be unable to get at it, although it still exists. Even recreating the partition will not allow you to get at the data.

4) Display Partition Data - This gives you a textual summary of the partitions on the disk so that you can see exactly what you have got.

Once the disk is partitioned it will then need to be formatted, see below, before it can be used.

LABEL

This allows you to alter, delete or apply a volume name to any disk. If you enter the command by itself then MS-DOS will assume that you mean the disk in the current drive. It will display the name, if any, that is presently applied to that disk and give you the option of deleting or changing it. Alternatively you can enter **LABEL [drive] [name]** and the name will be applied to the disk in Drive-A without you being told what is the current label. For the name you can use up to eleven of the accepted characters, including all the Extended ASCII set, i.e. but not the Reserved Characters.

MKDIR

To create a sub-directory you use this command, which stands for MaKe DIRectory, which can be abbreviated to just MD. The format for it is **MD [drive] [path] [name]**, However, whilst you can use it across drives, i.e. make a directory on Drive-C while logged onto Drive-E, it is more usual to use the command on the current drive.

Suppose you wanted to make a directory, on your current drive, called ALPHA. To do so you would enter **MD ALPHA** - it is that simple! If you then wanted to create a sub-directory called ONE within ALPHA you could enter **CD ALPHA**, to move into the first directory and providing you are on the drive in the first place, followed by **MD ONE**. Alternatively you could just enter **MD C:\ALPHA\ONE** and this would do it for you in a single operation.

Reserved Words

There are a number of words that are reserved by MS-DOS for its own purposes and you cannot therefore use them for naming files. (In addition there are some words that should be not be used because they have very specific connotations, e.g. command names.) If you find that you want to use any of these then you will have to use something else, you are not given a choice. The reserved words are;

AUX which is short for Auxiliary and it refers to the communications port into which you can connect a number of other devices, e.g. a modem.

BAS used as an extension; this is normally used by any program which is written in Basic.

BAT this is used as an extension for batch files.

COM refers to the communications serial port again and it is also used as the extension for certain programs.

CON is short for Console and it refers to the keyboard and/or the monitor.

EXE used as an extension for executable files.

LPT refers to the line printer parallel ports.

PRN also refers to the printer, see example in the text.

SYS reserved name for system files.

In addition to these words you also cannot use certain characters, either in the filename or the extension. These characters are: " $ * + = [ ] : ; | \ <, >. ? / and a blank space.

RMDIR

You cannot delete a directory using the DEL command. (If you try to delete a directory using DEL it will actually erase all the files that the directory contains.) Instead you have to use this one which is an abbreviation of ReMove DIRectory - it can be foreshortened to just RD. To use the command you just enter

RD [directory] and the directory will be removed. Note you cannot remove a directory that contains any files - you must delete all the files it contains first.

VOL

This will display the Volume label of the current disk or any disk that you specify. For instance if you enter VOL B: then you will be given the label that has been applied to that disk - always providing that you have a disk in the drive. If you leave off the drive letter then MS-DOS assumes that you mean the drive that you are currently logged on to.

Wildcards

A wildcard is a character that can be used to replace any other character or sequence of characters when used in conjunction with certain MS-DOS commands, e.g. COPY or DEL. There are only two such characters but their effects are considerable.

1) ? can be used to replace any individual character. Thus if you had four files named ALPHA.DOC, ALPHA.TXT, BETA.TXT and ALPHA.DOS and you wanted to copy the first and the last you would enter COPY ALPHA.DO? and they would be copied while the second and third ones would not. The question mark replaces the final character. To copy only those files with a.TXT extension you could enter **COPY ?????.TXT**. The question marks replace the first five characters.

2) However, instead of using a series of question marks you could use the second wildcard character, *. The asterisk is used to replace any sequence of characters. Thus to copy the files above you would enter **COPY *.TXT**. To copy all the files you would enter **COPY *.***.

Using the wildcards is something that takes a little practise, but makes using the command quicker from your point of view. For instance entering DEL *.* can delete all the files in the current directory, although you will be prompted to confirm that this is what you want in this case. The answer with the wildcards is to be careful with them - used abusively they can do an awful lot of damage to your files.

Disk Caches

A disk cache is a program that speeds up the data transfer rate. Basically it stores the name and locations of the most frequently used files and so MS-DOS can find them faster. Some caches operate slightly differently in that they actually hold entire files in memory. The important point to realise about caches is that they use up the computer's memory and ultimately this is the major deciding factor when you consider using one.

MS-DOS cannot use more than 640 Kb of memory as the primary work area. Although you can use any extra memory as a Ramdrive, this fundamental limit applies. Thus when you use the FILES and BUFFERS command you are eating into this limit and if you then use a memory resident program, that also grabs some of this base memory. Use too much of it and you will find that some of your application programs will not work correctly.

The disk cache resides between MS-DOS and the disk and it dramatically improves the apparent data access times because information is being shuffled around the RAM instead of having to go back and forth between the memory and the disk. However, the benefits it will give depend on the type of program being used. If you intend to use software that requires frequent disk access, e.g. a database, then you will notice an improvement. On the other hand if you are using a program that does not need to access the disk constantly then you are probably better off not using a cache because all it will do is reduce the amount of memory you have available for the application software. Ultimately it is your own personal preference.

There are a number of disk caches available, most of them are commercial programs but MS-DOS Version 3.30 comes with one of its own - Fastopen. In addition every version of MS-DOS comes with a pseudo-cache - the Buffers command.

BUFFERS

When you read information from the disk it is not sent directly to the application as you might expect, instead it is moved into an area of the RAM called a Buffer. This is because the amount of data in the Sector being read might not be complete, for example it may have an overspill into the next sector. Using the Buffers command dramatically increases the speed with which the computer can access data - it can be as much as 100 times faster than a pure disk read operation. The reason is that the RAM, where the data is now held, is purely electronic in operation and therefore ultra-fast when compared to a electro-mechanical disk. In essence the Buffers command acts as a poor computer's disk cache.

Each Buffer occupies 512 bytes of the RAM and generally this can be equated with a single disk sector, given that it is rare for sectors to be completely filled. As information is requested by a program it is read from the disk and placed into the Buffers. The next time you request information the computer checks the Buffer area first. If the information is already there then it is simply transferred to the program, thus speeding up the operation. If the information is not in the

Buffers then MS-DOS resorts to reading from the disk and overwrites the Buffers with the new information.

When you then perform a write operation the data is taken from the application program and placed into the Buffers - it does not go directly to the disk. Once the information has been safely placed into the Buffers it is then written to the disk. The reason for this is that you might well ask for the data back immediately. Again, it speeds up the access time. The overall result is that the Buffers always contain the latest data that has been read or written as they are cleared on the basis of first in, first out.

As mentioned, the Buffers command uses memory and you determine how large this area of memory will be by specifying the number of Buffers in the CONFIG.SYS using the line BUFFERS=n, where n is in the range 1 to 99 - although by default the machine will use 3 or 5 Buffers depending on the Version of MS-DOS being used. However, this default amount is never adequate. Generally speaking you will want to use between 20 and 30 Buffers depending on the application programs you are using. Theoretically you can improve the data access time by using a large number of Buffers but you can do the opposite and slow down the access time. The only way to find out which is correct for your machine is by trial and error.

FASTOPEN

FASTOPEN is only available as part of MS-DOS Version 3.30 and beyond. It is not a complete cache program but it does give you some of the benefits you would expect. It retains the data about the directory structure - keeping check of where the most used files are located so they can be accessed more rapidly than normal. The program has to be included in the AUTOEXEC.BAT file using the form FASTOPEN [drive] = n where [drive] is the logical drive whose information should be held and n is in the range 10 to 999 which refers to the number of files to be retained. Remember that if you change the AUTOEXEC.BAT you must reboot the machine for the change to become operable.

You can use FASTOPEN with as many logical drives as you possess but the number of files being held is the total. Thus if you used FASTOPEN [drive]=200 for drives C: to E: you would not have 600 files but 200. The number is the cumulative total. If you do want to use the command with a number of drives you can do so using a single line, e.g. FASTOPEN C:=200 D:=200 E:=200. Note that you cannot use the command with a floppy drive, and each entry requires 35 bytes. Thus using the command as above you will lose 7000 bytes of your RAM, i.e. 200*35. As with the Buffers command, you should experiment with different values until you get the one that provides the best performance.

Another point to bear in mind with FASTOPEN is that you cannot use it with any drive that has been used with JOIN, ASSIGN or APPEND. Equally, if you intend to use the command with a Ramdrive, then this must be created first, i.e.

before you use the FASTOPEN command, otherwise you are trying to use the command with a non-existent drive and this causes a hang-up of the system. Actually there is little point in using FASTOPEN with a Ramdrive, because the latter is already many times faster than a normal hard disk drive.

SMARTDRIVE

There are a large number of commercial disk caching programs available, far too many to cover here in depth. As they all possess the same basic operating parameters we will look at just one of them - Smartdrive. This program comes as part of the Windows program package and, in common with all caching programs, it is designed to reduce the amount of time that the computer spends reading the disk. Smartdrive is the only disk cache which will work properly in the Windows environment and it depends on there being Extended or Expanded memory available to it to use. As the majority of AT's come with 1 Mb of RAM, i.e. extended memory, there will be no problem using Smartdrive and allowing it to use the additional memory which lies above the MS-DOS 640 Kb limit.

Once it has been installed, generally as part of the Windows installation process, the program will run automatically every time you boot up the machine. It operates by taking the information from the disk and holding it in the memory ready for whichever program you are using to access. When you save a file it is first routed into the memory, to be held there in case it is wanted again, and then sent to the disk - in essence giving you two copies of the same file. As you unload a given application program, Smartdrive flushes any files that have been created by that program so that the space they were using is available for the next files.

You would expect that the data would remain in the memory until it was flushed on the basis of first in, first out, but this is not the case. Smartdrive was specially written to co-operate with Windows and provide the best possible solution for running Windows-based software. Thus it is assumed that if you want to move data from one program to another you would do so by having both applications open at once in separate windows. In this case there is no need for Smartdrive to retain the information from any one program once it has been closed.

Batch Files

Batch files are an integral part of using a computer and hard disk. Every computer will normally contain at least two batch files, the AUTOEXEC.BAT and CONFIG.SYS. The latter is not normally known as a batch file but in reality that is what it is, and both of these files will serve as an introduction to the subject. A batch file is simply a sequence of instructions, written in ASCII, such that the commands it contains will be operated or activated in serial order. They can range from the very simple to the exceedingly complex, but regardless of their complexity they are one of the most powerful tools you can use on a hard disk.

Batch files are essentially mini-programs and, as with any program, they have their own commands and rules of operation. In addition to using batch file specific commands, you can also include the names of any programs, with or without additional parameters, that are on the disk.

One of the most common and simplest uses of batch files is to run programs which are contained in sub-directories that are not mentioned in the PATH command, e.g. infrequently used software. As an example, consider the following file which might be used to run PC Outline. The lines have been numbered for clarity only, the numbers are not part of the batch file.

```
1 ECHO OFF
2 CLS
3 CD\PCO
4 PCO/Q
5 DEL *.BAK
6 CD\
7 CLS
```

Line 1 contains a batch file specific command, ECHO. Normally, whenever anything is executed on the computer, the machine gives you a running commentary of what it is doing by displaying, or echoing, its actions on the screen. This can be very useful, especially if the batch file is not working correctly and you need to pinpoint the mistake, but generally speaking you do not want it to happen. By including the line ECHO OFF the facility is disabled. Unfortunately the line itself is a command and thus it will be displayed, hence the need for Line 2 which clears the screen and the offending message.

If you are using MS-DOS Version 3.30 or greater you can combine the two lines by making use of an additional parameter to the ECHO command. By placing an 'at' sign, i.e. @, at the beginning of the first line the command will be automatically suppressed. Thus the line would then read @ECHO OFF and the second line could be discarded.

Line 3 is the one that changes directory for you. The command moves you from whatever directory you are currently logged onto and back to the root of the current drive. Then it moves down the directory structure to the sub-directory which contains the program you want to run. Note that you do not change drive, merely directory. If you wished to log onto another drive, you would need to include another line in the file which preceded Line 3 to access the required drive, e.g. D:.

Line 4 runs the program. The /Q parameter is a program one which suppresses the PC Outline startup screen. Once the program has been loaded you can use it as normal even though you are still within the batch file. Batch files normally occupy very little memory and so they will generally not cause any problems, especially if you are using non-memory hungry software. If you were wanting to use a program that needed lots of memory, e.g. WordStar, then you would not use a batch file to access it, instead you would include the directory which contains it in your PATH.

PC Outline can save files automatically as it is being run, using a timed device, with the result that the previous version of the file is resuffixed.BAK, the current version has the extension.PCO. The result is that you can end up with at least one file with this extension: if you open a number of files (the program allows up to 9 at once) then you can generate a large number of.BAK files. These occupy valuable disk space, as the cluster limitations apply to them, and therefore they are unlikely to be wanted. Line 5 deletes all such files once the program has been terminated and you return to the batch file.

Lines 6 and 7 then take you back to the root directory of the current drive and clears the screen.

Any non-PATH directory can be accessed in this way. In the normal course of events you would create a sub-directory to hold all your batch files and make that directory part of the PATH. Thus the files it contains could be accessed from anywhere on the disk. The advantage to doing this is that as you create more batch files they are automatically operable and can be used immediately.

The above file is an example of a non-interactive batch file, i.e. it just does what you request and gets on with it. But you can have batch files which are much more dynamic than that and which do more than just run programs. One of the simplest of these is the following:

```
ECHO OFF
CLS
%1
IF NOT EXIST IO.SYS GOTO NO
ECHO Disk %1 is bootable
GOTO END
:NO
ECHO Cannot boot from disk %1
:END
ECHO.
```

The purpose of this batch file is to check if any disk can be used for booting the machine and it is called ISIT.BAT. To use the file you enter ISIT [drive], i.e. you specify which drive you want the batch file to look at.

The first two lines are the same as the previous file. The third line is the important one. It makes use of the batch file ability to accept an input from you the user; that is what the

%1 means. In this case when you enter [drive], the designator you enter is used as this line - note that you must include the colon, e.g. C: or A:. Once the batch file reaches this line it will log onto the drive you have specified.

Line 4 checks to see if the disk concerned contains the hidden system file IO.SYS. Even though a file is hidden and does not appear on the DIR listing it is still there and the computer can recognise its existence. This line effectively says 'If a file named IO.SYS does not exist on the designated drive then miss out the next two lines of the batch file before continuing.' It makes use of two additional batch file commands.

IF is effectively a question. It can be used positively, i.e. to check if something is true, or negatively as here to check that something is false. The syntax of using the command is a bit backward but as long as it works....

GOTO is used to jump various lines of a batch file and you must include a named line for it to jump to. In this case it is labelled NO.

Line 5 will only be activated, i.e. the message it contains displayed, providing that the disk does contain a file called IO.SYS. If so then the message is echoed to the screen (note that it also informs you of the drive being tested because the %1 parameter does not change) and then the batch file continues to the next line. This contains a jump statement so that the file will ignore Lines 7 and 8.

Lines 7 and 9 are label lines. The colon that precedes the name tells the batch file that the line is a name and hence does not contain any commands that need to be activated. In the normal course of events any such line will be ignored. It is only when you have a jump, as in Line 6, that the file uses the names.

Line 8 displays a message which informs you that the disk, which will be named as in Line 5, is not a system disk. This will only be evoked if the statement in Line 4 is true, otherwise it will be ignored. Note that there is no jump statement after this line because it is placed near the end of the file and you want all the remaining lines to be activated

The final line will display a blank line before returning you to the system prompt, providing it is entered exactly as written.

You could make the batch file more informative by including REM statements. These are lines that contain comments for your benefit only and which the computer ignores. Thus the file could look like this:

```
REM Disable the echoing facility
ECHO OFF

REM Clear the screen of the
previous statement
CLS

REM Log onto the drive as input
REM when the batch file was
REM invoked
%1
```

```
REM Check to see if the hidden
REM file is included on the disk
REM being checked
IF NOT EXIST IO.SYS GOTO NO

REM The disk does contain the
REM hidden file and thus we want
REM a message to that effect
ECHO Disk %1 is bootable

REM Miss the next two lines
GOTO END

REM Name line for a disk not
REM containing the system files
:NO

REM Display the appropriate
REM message
ECHO Cannot boot from this disk
%1

REM Name line for end of file
:END

REM Display a blank line
ECHO.

REM Program terminates back to
REM the system prompt.
REM Remember that we are now
REM logged onto the drive
REM specified when the file was
REM invoked.
```

The trouble with this is that you tend to get lost in the REM statements and so you have to include blank lines - and don't forget that both of these occupy disk space. The file as it now stands occupies 843 bytes as opposed to the original which has only 132 bytes. While REM statements can be of use in very large batch files it is questionable whether they are necessary in short files such as the original of the above.

One problem that will occur with ISIT.BAT is that it does not check to ensure it is in the root directory of the disk being tested. Thus, if you run it within a sub-directory other than the root, you will find that the message on Line 8 is displayed - because the system files are always in the Root directory. This problem can be fixed by inserting an extra line between Lines 3 and 4 containing the command CD\ which ensures you are in the Root.

The only way to learn to use batch files is to play with them, experiment to find what they are capable of and what they cannot do. Everyone knows how to write simple batch files, like the AUTOEXEC.BAT, but very few people ever bother to develop the skill required to write the more complex ones.

Batch File Commands

CALL

This is only available in MS-DOS Version 3.30 and beyond. Its purpose is to allow you to run a second batch file from within another - something that is not easy in earlier versions of MS-DOS. With earlier versions of MS-DOS you had to create a command shell if you wanted to use a second batch file or have it only mentioned at the end so that it ran sequentially. However, with this new command you can now run a second file and temporarily suspend the first before returning to it.

CLS

As mentioned previously, this command simply clears the screen of extraneous detail and leaves it blank.

COMMAND

In versions of MS-DOS earlier than 3.30 you had to use this command to evoke a shell so that a second batch file could be run. The second batch file runs in the command shell which is then revoked once the second batch file terminates and you return to the original.

ECHO

Used to display messages on the monitor. Can also be used to (de)activate the echoing of command operations on the screen.

ERRORLEVEL

An errorlevel is a numeric code, in the range 0 to 255, that can be generated by certain operations. It is actually created by some programs as a result of their actions. You can use this code within a batch file to display conditional messages. For example by using the statement IF ERRORLEVEL n [message], or you can use it to generate other commands by using IF ERRORLEVEL n [command].

One problem that occurs with errorlevels is that they are hierarchical. That is to say ERRORLEVEL 1 means any errorlevel with a value of 1 or greater, thus errorlevel 255 will activate the command or message. Therefore if you intend to use a number of errorlevel lines in a batch file you have to place them in descending order, e.g.

```
IF ERRORLEVEL 3 [action]
IF ERRORLEVEL 2 [action]
IF ERRORLEVEL 1 [action]
```

GOTO

The jump statement which must include a valid label as the position within the file that the program is to vault to.

IF

The conditional inquisitor, i.e. it is used to check the validity of statements. It can also be used to check the falseness of statements by placing NOT immediately after the word as in the second batch file above.

MORE

Is a condition of a filter, check your MS-DOS manual for details of these. It must be preceded by |, the symbol above the backslash on most keyboards. Filters can be extremely powerful and they are used to generate a specific result.

PAUSE

Causes the batch file to halt until any key is pressed, e.g. to allow you to change a floppy disk. When the batch file reaches this line it will display a message on the screen and then wait for your response.

REM

Abbreviation for Remark or Reminder. Any line preceded by this word will be ignored in the operation of the batch file.

SET

Displays the variables that you have enacted, e.g. the PATH. You can also use this command directly from the system prompt.

SHIFT

Used in conjunction with the % parameters. Because you are limited to using 10 such parameters, numbered 0 to 9, you may find that you need to move them along and so free the last one for additional input - although this is rare.

Chapter 8
Front Ends

Introduction

While MS-DOS is probably the most widely used operating system in the world, it cannot be said that it is user-friendly. In order to use it properly you must know the name of the commands, their parameters and their foibles. Once the computer has been booted up, all that confronts you is a thin flashing cursor which sits there waiting for you to input a command. Many people find this intimidating and there can be little doubt that the unfriendliness of MS-DOS has contributed significantly to the myth that computers are complex, difficult to use and only for the initiated. In fact nothing could be further from the truth. A computer, regardless of whether it is a PC, XT or AT, is nothing more or less than a high speed calculating machine, albeit with mass storage abilities. It can do nothing except add and subtract! In reality it is not the computer that is complex; it is the software that it uses which is apparently enigmatic and mysterious. But even here, there are only three basic program types:

1) Text manipulation programs; such as word processors, DTP programs or idea organisers.

2) Data manipulation programs; including databases, menu programs, communications programs, utility programs, etc.

3) Arithmetic manipulation programs; encompassing spreadsheets, financial packages, graphics packages, etc.

Even then the first two could be amalgamated into one type. Not everyone will agree with these definitions - especially anyone who has an interest in propagating and maintaining the mythology of the computer expert. Be all that as it may, the user, particularly someone who is relatively new to computers, still has to get the programs up and running. As you progress and acquire experience, so the system prompt becomes less intimidating but initially you may well find that it is a good idea to make use of a front end program - alternatively called a menu.

Menus come in all shapes, sizes and capabilities, ranging from simple alternative directory display programs to complete infrastructures like Windows. Many menu programs can be classed as utilities, the level of applicability varies enormously though, and they provide a host of extra file management commands which MS-DOS itself is lacking.

In the following pages is a brief look at some such programs. They have purposely been chosen because they provide a good indication of the range of menu programs available, but they should not be taken as totally comprehensive. (For example there are over 100 Shareware menu programs. To cover all of them in detail would require a complete series of books which is impractical at the moment.)

XTree

Xtree and Xtree Professional are hard disk Front Ends. In other words they are programs to make finding your way around a hard disk or disks easier. Most people who have come across Xtree will have done so through the purchase of a Western Digital Filecard, the generic name for a series of hard cards of various capacities. That is where I first found it. It is certainly the piece of software which is used more often than any other on my machine, although now I have Xtree Professional, which is well worth the money. They are both published by Executive Software in the USA and are available from certain retailers in the UK. Xtree Professional is the one we shall be taking an in depth look at here.

Firstly, XTPROCFG allows you to modify all sorts of parameters including telling it where it lives on your machine. Xtpro prefers to live in its own directory, and this is essential if you want to use it to its fullest advantage. Also modifiable are the colours it uses - well worth playing with. I also prefer to run it from within a batch file and use the /R switch which logs it into the root directory of the drive.

The first thing you see when the program is invoked is that the screen is split into several windows. The two main ones are horizontal: the top one is the Directory window, the bottom one is the Files window.

The Directory Window

This shows the directory structure of the disk. The root directory is at the top of the list, and all other directories are sorted alphabetically and displayed from the top of the window to the bottom. Main directories are on the left, with sub-directories indented to the right. If you have used the /R then the cursor bar will also be located on the root directory. The window containing the highlight bar or cursor is the currently active one: Enter swaps between the active and inactive windows.

To begin with, the Directory Window is active and the highlight bar is at the root directory. This may be moved to any directory on the disk using the cursor keys.

File Window

There are four file windows. The Small File and the Expanded Windows list the files found in the current directory. The Showall Window lists all files on the current drive and the Global Window lists all files on all logged drives. If you swap now to the file window, the highlight bar indicates the current file. This is the file which will be affected by file commands. The highlight bar is moved with the cursor keys.

Multiple-file commands will affect all tagged files that match the file specification in the current directory if the Small Files Window or Expanded Window is active, on the current drive if the Showall Window is active, or on all logged drives if the Global Window is active. The return key toggles between the directory, small and large file windows. The cursor keys, Page keys, and Home and End keys move the highlight bar from item to item within a window or scroll a window.

Special movement is possible in the Directory Window. The Right key moves down the current path to the last sub-directory in that path. Left moves to the parent of the current directory, stopping when the parent is the first-level sub-directory. Tab moves down to the next directory on the same level as the current directory, within the same branch of the tree. Shift-Tab moves up to the next directory on the same level as the current directory, within the same branch of the tree.

File Specifications

File specs are where Xtpro is very powerful. In either window you can ask for file specification with the F. The command line at the bottom of the screen will clear and you will be prompted to input a file specification. You can enter up to four file specifications by separating each one with a comma, e.g. *.EXE, *.COM, W*.TXT. This would only show files that have a.EXE or.COM or start with a W and have a.TXT extension. Files that meet the file Specification are referred to as Matching files. (When XTree is first started, the *.* wildcard specification appears and all files are available to the program.) This enables you to view combinations of files. When the length of a multiple file specification exceeds the space available in the File Specification Box, a right arrow indicates that part of the file specification is not visible.

Disk

This identifies the current drive, and shows the volume label and available bytes for this disk. This changes each time you log or select a new drive. Log keeps the information for previously logged drives in memory and Alt/Log releases all other drives. Use the keypad + and - keys to select a previously logged drive without relogging it.

Statistics

When the Directory Window or Showall Window is active, the statistics in this box give the space available for the entire disk. When the Small File Window is active, these apply only to the current directory. When the Global Window is active, the statistics include all logged disks. The Total statistics let you see the total number of files and how much space these files use. The Matching statistics indicate how many files match the File Specification and the amount of space they utilise. The Tagged statistics show how many files have been tagged (marked with a diamond) for multiple-file operations and how many bytes these tagged files occupy.

Finally, this box displays the name of the current directory if the Directory window is active or the current file if any of the file windows is active.

Function Keys

Xtree uses certain of the function and other keys to provide some shortcuts and help.

F1 Accesses Xtree Help at any time.

F2 Activates the Destination Directory Window. This is only available when being prompted for a destination path during a copy or move command.

F9 An alternative to holding down the Ctrl key, followed by a command key to invoke Ctrl commands.

F10 Alternative to holding down the Alt key. Press F10 followed by a command key to invoke Alt commands.

Esc Cancels an operation.

+ Selects the next logged disk. Display information from memory.

- Selects the previous logged disk. Display information from memory.

Home and End Move the cursor to the beginning or end of the line.

Left and Right Move the cursor one position to the left or right without altering the text.

Insert Toggle insert on and off. When insert is on, the cursor is displayed as a block and typing inserts characters to the left of the cursor. When insert is off, the cursor is displayed as an underline and typing causes the character under the cursor to be replaced.

Ctrl/Backspace Erase the line and move the cursor to the beginning.

Backspace Delete one character to the left of the cursor. Characters to the right are moved to the left.

Enter Complete the editing and begin processing.

Destination Directory Window

With this feature you point to a destination directory rather than typing the path when moving or copying files. This is accessed by using F when being asked for the destination path during a copy or move operation. The highlight bar identifies the destination directory. Use the cursor keys to highlight the desired directory. Press F2 or Enter to select the directory and 'feed' the path name to the destination prompt. Press Esc to return to the destination prompt without feeding a path name. Originally, the directory structure of the current disk was displayed. Display a previously logged drive with the keypad + and - keys. You may also log another drive without releasing currently logged drives with the Log command.

Directory Commands

There are three Directory Command Menus: Standard, Ctrl and Alt. The standard ones are:

Available Show space available on any disk.

Delete Remove the current directory.

Filespec Select a new file specification for XTree operations.

Global Display all matching files on all logged drives.

Log disk Log another disk without releasing disks which were previously logged.

Makedir Make a new sub-directory under the current directory.

Print Print directory information on the printer.

Rename Rename the current directory.

Showall Display all matching files on the current drive.

Tag Tag all matching files in the current directory.

Untag Untag all matching files in the current directory.

Volume Change the disk volume label.

eXecute Run a program or MS-DOS command without releasing disks.

Quit Quit Xtree and return to MS-DOS.

The Ctrl Directory Commands are called by holding down Ctrl and pressing the first upper-case letter of the command name.

Global Display all matching tagged files on all logged drives.

Showall Display all matching tagged files on the current drive.

Tag Tag all matching files on the current drive.

Untag Untag all matching files on the current drive.

Finally the Alt Directory Commands which are activated by pressing Alt and then the first upper-case letter of the command name activates the following:

File Change the format and amount of file information displayed in the File Windows.

Log disk Log another disk and release all disks which were previously logged.

Release disk Release (unlog) a disk.

Sort criteria Change the criteria used for sorting the file display.

Tag Tag any file on the disk whose file attributes match a specified setting.

Untag Remove the tag from any file on the disk whose file attributes match a specified setting.

eXecute Run a program or MS-DOS command, releasing all disks.

File Commands

There are three File Command Menus: Standard, Ctrl and Alt. These commands are available from the Small, Expanded, and Showall File Windows. A subset of these commands is available from the Global File Window. The standard commands are:

Attributes Modify the attributes of the current file.

Copy Copy the current file to a new disk and/or path.

Delete Delete the current file.

Edit Create or edit a text file.

Filespec Select a group of files for XTrees operations.

Log disk Log a disk without releasing previously logged disks.

Move Move the current file to a different directory.

Print Print the contents of the current file.

Rename Rename the current file.

Tag Tag the current file.

Untag Remove the tag from the current file.

View View the contents of the current file on the screen.

eXecute - Execute a program without releasing logged disks.

The Ctrl commands will operate on several files at once. The files affected by these commands are those files which match the File Specification and are tagged; located in the current directory if the Files Window is active, on the current drive if the Showall window is active, or on all logged drives if the Global Window is active. To use these commands, hold down Ctrl, which displays the Ctrl File Commands Menu, and press the appropriate key.

Attribute Modify the attributes of the tagged files.

Copy Copy the tagged files to a new disk and/or path.

Delete Delete the tagged files.

Move Move the tagged files to another directory. (This is not available from the Global File Window).

Print Print the contents of the tagged files.

Rename Rename the tagged files.

Tag Tag the matching files.

Untag Remove the tag from the matching files.

To access the Alt commands, hold down the Alt key, which displays the Alt File Commands Menu, and press a key.

Copy Copy tagged files to another disk, keeping each file in the same directory on the destination as it is in on the source disk. The destination directory is created if it does not exist.

File Change the format and amount of file information displayed in the File Window.

Log disk Log a disk and release other logged disks.

Release Release (unlog) a disk.

Sort Change the criteria for sorting the file display.

Tag Tag files according to attribute settings.

Untag Untag files according to attribute settings.

eXecute Execute a program and release all logged disks.

Quit Leave Xtree and return to MS-DOS to the directory which is current in XTree.

Delete Directory

Removes the current directory from the current disk. Xtree, like MS-DOS will not allow you delete a directory which still contains files or sub directories.

Global Files Window

The Global File Window overlays the Directory and Small File Windows. Only files with names matching the File Specification are shown and are affected by XTree's operations.

When the highlight bar is in the Global Files Window, it is active and XTree's Global File Commands may be used. The highlight bar indicates the current file. This is the file which will be affected by Standard file commands (those not preceded by the Ctrl or Alt keys). Move the highlight bar with the cursor keys. Multiple-file commands will affect all tagged files that match the file specification in all directories on all logged drives.

Global Lists files in all directories on all logged drives.

Ctrl Lists tagged files in all directories on all logged drives.

Log disk

Reads the file and directory information for a drive from the disk and changes the current drive for further Xtree operations. This command is available from the Directory Window or any of the file Windows. You are prompted for the new drive to log. The file and directory information for that drive is then read from disk and the disk statistics are updated to reflect the new disk.

Log Logs a new drive and retains information for all previously logged drives in memory. To unlog a specific drive, select the Alt/ Release command.

Alt-L Logs a new drive and releases all previously logged drives.

Makedir

Creates a sub-directory under the current directory. You will be prompted for the name of the new directory which must follow the normal MS-DOS rules. The window will be updated to show the new directory in the directory structure.

Print Directory

There are three options available from the Directory Window. The first prints a list of all tagged files on the current drive organised by sub-directory. The second prints a list of all path names on the current drive. Finally the last prints a graphic representation of the directory structure for the current drive.

Rename Directory

Changes the name of the current directory. Xtree prompts for the new name. The name must follow the normal rules for valid MS-DOS file names. The directory is renamed and the Directory window is updated to show the new name.

Showall File Window

The Showall File Window overlays the Directory and Small File Windows. Only those files with names matching the file specification are shown and are affected by XTree's operations. When the highlight bar is in the Showall File Window, it is active and Xtree's File Commands may be used. This is the file which is affected by Standard file commands (those not preceded by the Ctrl or

Alt keys). Move the highlight bar with the cursor keys.

Volume

Changes the volume label name of the current drive. Enter a new name following MS-DOS rules for volume labels. A volume name cannot be the same as the name of a file or sub-directory in the root directory. If you do use a volume name MS-DOS will not allow you to do a format until you enter the volume name correctly.

The version of XTREE covered above contains all the standard functions and commands that you will find in most versions of the program. However, there are minor differences between them.

Windows 3

Regardless of whether you like it or not, and it has to be said that many people don't like it, MS-DOS is the most widely used operating system in the world - the system is used on approximately 40 million computers world-wide. The operating system controls every aspect of the computer, not just the disk drives, and it does so without you, the user, even noticing. For all that, MS-DOS does have one major problem - it is very unfriendly, or apparently so. When you turn on the computer, it runs through its in-built tests, loads the operating system, runs your tailoring files, the CONFIG.SYS and AUTOEXEC.BAT, and then sits there... waiting.... All you can see is a little cursor flashing away rhythmically on an otherwise blank screen. Not the most inspiring introduction to the joys of computing.

In addition MS-DOS has remained largely unchanged since its original inception. Because it has to remain downwards compatible, which simply means that it must be able to run any software that was written for a previous version, it becomes limited in what it can do. Since the original IBM PC there have been enormous advances in the chip technology; firstly to the 80286, then the 80386 and now to 80486 - and the 80586 is due before the end of 1990. But MS-DOS still has to operate as if the computer was an 8086 - it cannot take advantage of the enhancements and improvements in the chip design and technology. So what can be done? The answer is to work around the problem.

Because they realised that many people are intimidated by the operating system, Microsoft developed a new product that used pictures, called Icons, instead. The system is called Windows and it is known as a GUI system. The acronym means Graphical User Interface and is simply techno-speak for a system that uses images on screen rather than a system prompt. The User bit refers to you, and the Interface is the visual aspect of the program with which you interact. (There are probably more acronyms in the computer industry than anywhere else, and new ones are created almost every day.) A GUI system has been used as the basis of all Apple computers, IBM's main competitor, since their launch.

Windows presents you with a series of Icons, essentially little pictures, of programs, files, disks, etc. and you use a Mouse and Pull-down Menus to select and run the software that you want to use, hence the name WIMP (Windows, Icons, Mouse and Pull-down Menus) environment. One major advantage of the system is that once you master Windows you essentially know how to use 80% of any software that has been designed to run under the environment. Because Windows provides a consistent interface for the software, there will be only minor differences between various packages - their overall performance and use will remain unchanged. The advantage of this is that it provides a consistency and friendliness that is lacking under pure MS- DOS.

There have been three versions of Windows and each one has been a response to an improvement in the hardware available. The first version ran on the original PC and its cousins, i.e. those which used an 8088 or 8086 microchip. The next version was used mainly on 80286 machines which, appropriately enough, was called Windows/ 286. (There was a version for 80386 machines, called Windows/386, but not many people used it, preferring to use Windows/286 for a number of reasons which we'll not go into here.) The latest version is intended to run on 80386 machines and it is the best yet. It is quick and easy to use, simple and intuitive.

Windows 3 is the most fundamentally important software development since the inception of the original IBM PC and the creation of MS-DOS. It brings to MS-DOS a degree of power and control that has been lacking for some time. Windows 3 is a bright, colourful, intuitive environment from which to run any and all software - including that which is designed to run under MS-DOS. Windows 3 is, quite simply, superb.

Windows 3 is a system so far advanced from the earlier versions that they might as well be two different products for all that they look similar. Windows 3 provides full and total support for the 80386 microchip and its ability to control memory - the fundamentally limiting factor of any computer. It is now possible to have full concurrency using Windows. This means that, providing you have sufficient memory, you can effectively run a number of programs as if each was running on a separate PC - all on one machine. This ability is limited only by the amount of RAM that is installed in the computer on which the system is being run. Windows 3 is what Windows always should have been and further demonstrates Microsoft's commitment to end users.

Windows 3 does much more than provide the end user, i.e. you, with a standardised interface: that is just the surface gloss. Beneath this colourful exterior the heart of the system has been radically changed. For example, Windows 3 is downwards compatible with previous versions of Windows only in a very limited sense. The new program can run software from the earlier versions, but only in one particular way - in Real mode, see below. Windows 3 is that rare thing in the computer industry - an upgrade that is so radically better than the original it almost severs its connections with the earlier version.

Windows in general, and Windows 3 in particular, allows you to transfer images and text from one application to another with ease and so you can create a complex document using source material from a range of different software. Simply select the item you want in one application, copy it to the Clipboard, open the next application and paste the data into place. Because of the way in which Windows 3 works you can do this even from MS-DOS programs. Windows 3 allows you to open an MS-DOS window, effectively causing Windows to retreat into the memory, and operate the computer as if Windows wasn't there - although you do have to be careful about memory usage in such a case. You can then run any program as you would have done if you did not have Windows installed. When you have finished you simply enter EXIT and this will reinstate Windows onto the screen, fully operable and ready to go.

Operating Modes

When it comes to the actual hardware that the program is running on, Windows 3 really comes into its own. Windows 3 provides three different methods of operation, known as Modes, and these have a fundamental effect on how the computer works. Each mode is dependent on certain hardware parameters being present. The modes are:

Real Mode forces the chip, regardless of whether it is an 80286, 80386, 80386SX or 80486, to operate in an identical way to the 8086 chip that was the heart of the original IBM PC. This means that it can run standard MS-DOS software without any modifications to the programs. Any program running in Real mode can access a maximum of 1 Mb of RAM. If you are using software that was developed for an earlier version of Windows then the only way that you can use that software without encountering any problems is to use this mode. On any machine that has 1 Mb or less of RAM you can only run Windows 3 in Real mode. If the machine has 1 Mb or less of RAM and you enter WIN, then Real Mode is what you will get. Windows 3 can be told to run in Real mode on any machine that has more than 1 Mb of RAM and you do so by entering WIN/R from the system prompt when you activate the Windows program. It is imperative that if you are using Windows-based software from an earlier version of Windows, e.g. Windows/286, that you run Windows 3 in Real Mode or you are likely to encounter all kinds of strange and/ or possibly disastrous problems.

Standard Mode is fully compatible with the 80286 microchip Protected mode and it is in this mode that Windows 3 is normally likely to run on most machines. In many ways Standard Mode is the best of the three - it certainly appears to run faster and is more responsive that the other two. In this mode Windows has access to extended memory and it will allow you to switch between non-Windows programs, i.e. programs which run under pure MS-DOS - provided you have enough memory to do so. For example, one of the machines that this book is being written on is an 80386 AT with 2 Mb of RAM. Because 256 Kb is used for SMARTDRV.SYS, the Windows disk caching program, and 768 Kb is used for a Ramdrive, which provides the print buffer for Windows, there is insufficient memory to allow switching between MS-DOS programs from within the Windows environment. I can switch from Windows to MS-DOS and back again, but I cannot have two or more MS-DOS programs open at the same time. If I try to do so the machine locks up tight and needs to be rebooted. (Mind you, that could well be the machine's fault rather than Windows'.)

386-Enhanced Mode is brand new and this is what makes Windows 3 so special. Put simply, it allows Windows 3 to operate on an 80386, 80386SX or 80486 chip in such a way that it simulates the Real mode of the 8086. It does this by using the Virtual Memory capabilities of these three chips which will allow programs, in this case Windows 3, to use more memory than is actually present by creating pseudo-memory using the hard disk.

When in this mode Windows 3 can perform genuine multi-tasking of either specific Windows application and/or of MS-DOS programs. Each program operates independently of the others and each is allocated its own 1 Mb chunk of the available RAM. In essence this means that you can have a number of programs all running on the same machine, in tandem with and yet separate from each other, i.e. you can apparently have multiple PC's on the same machine.

Note, however, that if the machine possesses less than 4 Mb of RAM then the multi-tasking will be severely limited or even nonexistent. In a sense, the amount of RAM available will have a direct bearing on the number of programs that can be multi- tasked, as each one will require 1 Mb for its own use. Thus if you have 4 Mb you can have four programs running simultaneously, 8 Mb gives you eight and so on. (In fact you can do slightly better but the principle remains the same.) 386-Enhanced mode will only operate by default if your system hardware matches the specification required of it, see below. However you can force the program to run in this mode on a machine with less than the optimum system resources, by entering WIN/3 at the system prompt. The problem with this though, is that the program is very likely to run appreciably slower than if it was in Standard mode on the same machine.

Each mode places a limit on the minimum hardware requirements as follows:

To run in Real mode you need a minimum of 640 Kb of RAM.

To run in Standard mode you need a computer based on the 80286 chip or better plus a minimum of 1 Mb of RAM - though the more memory you have, the better.

For 386-Enhanced mode you must have an 80386, 80386SX or 80486 plus an absolute minimum of 2 Mb of free RAM although 4 Mb of memory is better.

In addition, regardless of what mode you will be using, you must also have the following:

a) A hard disk with at least 15 Mb, and preferably twice that, of free capacity.

b) At least one floppy drive.

c) A Mouse. You can use Windows without a Mouse but it's like trying to dig without a spade - possible but very exhausting and, ultimately, not worth the effort.

System Resources

People tend to forget that a computer is nothing more nor less that a tool, in exactly the same way as a hammer or a lawn-mower: it simply allows you to do certain things better and more efficiently than using something else, try hammering in nails with a half brick and you'll see what I mean. Equally try doing word processing with a typewriter - it is not possible, you must use a computer. However, there is this odd myth about computers - they are complex, frighteningly fast, superhuman, and awkward to use. This myth contains a grain of truth but it is only partially true. Yes, they are complex, but the complexities are hidden away and have little or no relevance to the user; they are fast, but speed is not everything, if anything a computer is merely an idiot savant - processing numbers at a rapid pace but the numbers mean nothing to it.

Every computer has a number of component parts - the system resources - and Windows 3 makes full and complete use of them. The system resources can be broken down into three main types:

a) Chips
b) Memory
c) Disk Drives

Each resource has its own limitations and problems but Windows 3 goes a long way towards smoothing out the incompatibilities between the resources and it helps to integrate them into a cohesive whole. But getting them right can be a problem. Windows 3 is the most important software development of the decade and it is pushing hardware sales in a way that no other software package has ever done.

If nothing else the type of chip you are using and the amount of memory you have available will have a marked effect on how Windows operates.

80386+ Modes

Real Mode forces the chip to operate in an identical way, albeit faster, than the original 8086 chip. In fact it makes the chip operate as an 80286. This means that it can run standard MS-DOS software without any modifications to the programs. Any program running in Real mode can only access 1 Mb of RAM.

Protected Mode is fully compatible with the 80286 Protected Mode, i.e. the mode that theoretically allows the chip to multi-task.

Virtual Real Mode is new and specific to the 80386 and later chips. It allows the chip to run with program memory protection but it simulates the Real mode of the 8086. In this mode the chip can perform genuine multi-tasking. Each standard MS-DOS program operates independently of the others and each is allocated its own 1 Mb chunk of the available RAM. In essence this means that you can have a number of programs all running on the same machine, in tandem with and yet separate from each other, i.e. you can apparently have multiple PC's on the same machine.

Note, however, that if the machine only possesses 1 Mb of RAM then the multi-tasking will be severely limited or even nonexistent. In a sense the amount of RAM available will have a direct bearing on the number of programs that can be multi-tasked as each one will require 1 Mb for its own use. Thus if you have 4 Mb you can have 4 programs running simultaneously, 8 Mb gives you 8 and so on. (In fact you can do slightly better than that but the principle remains the same.)

Windows 3 takes advantage of the way that the 80386 can use different modes of operation. Windows Real mode is identical to the chip's Real mode, Windows Standard mode uses the Protected mode, and 386-Enhanced uses Virtual Real mode.

Any AT based on the 80386 is a powerful machine and this is reflected by the storage media it uses. Most 80386 based machines will have a 70 Mb hard disk as a minimum, 120 Mb is commonplace and 320 Mb plus is not unusual. The machines will normally have 2 Mb of RAM as a minimum, more usually 4 Mb, and sometimes 8 Mb. High density floppy drives, either 5.25" 1.2 Mb, 3.5" 1.44 Mb or both is the norm. In addition the majority of these machines will use a SVGA (Super Video Graphics Array) monitor that gives high definition and multiple colours. I would regard a machine based on the 80386 with at least 4 Mb of RAM, a 70 Mb hard drive and an SVGA monitor as the absolute minimum needed to run Windows 3 properly.

Memory Types

RAM, Random Access Memory, is a fundamental part of the computer system, indeed it could be said that it is the most fundamental part of the computer system, without it nothing will work. There are three kinds of memory available and which you use, and how you use them, will directly affect how Windows operates.

Conventional memory is found on every computer. The maximum amount of conventional memory that can be fitted to any computer is 640 Kb - although some machines come with only 512 Kb of RAM. Generally speaking it is only low level machines, e.g those based on the 8088 or 8086 chips, which have such a limited amount of memory. MS-DOS uses this conventional memory for running, in fact the operating system itself uses a sizable chunk of it with the result that you may well find that you have a maximum free memory capacity of less than 550 Kb even before you load any other programs - although this depends on which version of MS-DOS you are using. For example, Version 3.3 takes much less space than does Version 4.01 and Version 5.0 makes up even less.

Extended memory is that part of the RAM which extends above the 640 Kb limit. For example, most AT computers come complete with 2 Mb of RAM. 640 Kb of this is Conventional memory and the remaining 1408 Kb is Extended memory. You can also increase the amount of Extended memory by installing an add-on board into one of the vacant slots on the computer - although it has to be said that these tend to be expensive - or you can usually increase the amount of memory by installing additional chips directly into the motherboard. Extended memory is vitally important to Windows 3, the more extended memory you have the better Windows 3 will work. If you intend using Windows 3 as your default operating system shell then I strongly recommend that you increase the amount of extended memory you have so that you have at least 4 Mb of RAM. By doing so you will notice a marked improvement in Windows' performance, speed and dynamism.

Expanded memory is different to the previous two, in more senses than one. Such memory is normally always board mounted, so that it fits into an expansion slot, and it requires a special program so that the computer can use it. The majority of Expanded memory boards conform to a standard known as LIM, which is simply the initial letters of the three companies that developed the standard, namely Lotus, Intel and Microsoft. One advantage of Expanded memory boards is that they can be configured so that they act as Extended memory, Expanded memory or both.

Windows 3 works best with Extended memory, although some Windows applications can work with Expanded memory. The amount of memory you have available has a direct effect on the way that Windows will operate.

With less than 1 Mb of RAM, Windows can only run in Real mode, i.e. the slowest and least dynamic method of operation. Even if your machine is an 80286 or 80386 based one it will still only run in Real mode if there is insufficient memory.

With between 1 Mb and 2 Mb of RAM, Windows can run in either Real or Standard mode on an 80286 or 80386 machine and by default it will run in the latter. (You cannot use Standard Mode on an 8088 or 8086 based machine.) However this depends on how the memory is allocated. If you have a number of memory resident programs loaded, and thus consuming memory, there may not be enough left for Windows to run in Standard mode - you must have at least 1 Mb of RAM free and available to run in Standard mode. Because the modes are downwards compatible, if you can run Standard mode you can also run in Real mode.

With more than 2 Mb of RAM, the type of chip being used becomes the deciding factor. If you had an 80286 machine with 16 Mb of RAM, Windows will still only work in Standard mode - because that is all the chip is capable of. However, if you have an 80386SX or better with even 2 Mb of RAM you can run Windows in 386-Enhanced mode. Note, this mode is only available on an 80386SX, 80386 or 80486 based machine - all of which will allow Windows 3 to run in any of the three modes.

The type of disk drive you are using does have an effect on how Windows operates, especially if you are using an 80286 machine. Many Windows applications constantly read to and write from the disk, especially those programs from third party manufacturers like CorelDRAW. In fact CorelDRAW is the most disk intensive software that I know of! In addition the printer spooler can use the hard disk as temporary storage, to hold files before they are actually sent to the printer, and this very effectively slows down Windows programs because the disk is trying to serve too many masters. However, a fast disk drive does help to alleviate this problem. To speed up the printing you should use a Ramdrive - providing you have sufficient memory to create a decent sized one, i.e. at least 1 Mb.

When Windows is running in 386-Enhanced mode, and only then, it can simulate memory by using the hard disk and creating a swapfile, a special file which is used exclusively by Windows, although actually you originate it. The swapfile can be huge: it can be anything up to half the free space of your hard disk. Once the file has been created it remains on the hard disk until you remove it, although it does not appear when you enter DIR because it is a hidden, system file. Because Windows regards the swapfile as an extension of memory you can end up with a report which tells you that you have, for example, 8,096 Mb of free RAM on a machine that has only got 2 Mb of RAM to start with. The advantage is that Windows runs much faster, however the type of disk being used does have a marked effect on the speed of the swapping.

With Windows running in Real or Standard mode, the program creates temporary application swapfiles, i.e. it doesn't use the swapfile mentioned above. Once you terminate Windows all these temporary files will be deleted.

Summary

- Your system resources have a definite effect on how Windows operates on your machine.

- Windows 3 must have an 80386SX or better to function in 386-Enhanced Mode. This mode is not available on 80286 machines.

- Conventional memory is that part of the RAM up to 640 Kb.

- Extended memory is that part of the RAM above the 640 Kb MS-DOS limit, which is installed in the machine. The more extended memory you have, the better Windows 3 will work.

- Expanded memory is board mounted and is intended to allow you to increase the amount of memory you have, quickly and easily. Memory boards must conform to the LIM standard to work with Windows 3.

- Neither the type of chip nor the type of disk interface you are using seems to make any really noticeable difference to Windows' performance but the amount of memory you have available does make a striking difference.

Basic Layout

Every Windows application contains certain elements that are common to them all and this allows the programs to operate in essentially the same way using those elements. Along the top of every Windows application are four common elements; the Control Box, the Title Bar, the Minimise button and the Maximise button.

The Control Box, a square with a horizontal line in it at the top right hand corner of the window, contains a list of commands that control how the window that bears the application operates or appears. The commands it contains are common to all Windows applications and they are as follows. All the Control Box commands can be activated directly from the keyboard using **Alt-Space-[underlined letter]** or you can use the mouse to click on the Control Box and then again on the command you want to use.

Restore This will return the window to its original size and shape after the window has been reduced to an icon, i.e. minimised. The command will also return a window to its former size after it has been maximised, i.e. enlarged to cover the entire screen.

Move This command allows you to move a non-maximised window or an icon around the screen so that you can position it where you want it to be. The command is really one to use from the keyboard because using a mouse enables you to drag the image yourself.

Size This allows you to change the size of the window. Normally you would only use this command from the keyboard because you can much more easily change the size of a window using the mouse.

Minimise This command allows you to shrink any open window down to an icon, a pictorial representation of the program, which will then appear at the bottom of the screen. Using a mouse you simply click on the Minimise button to get the same effect. To return an icon to an active window you can either use the Restore command, above, or just double click on the icon you want.

Maximise This is the opposite of the previous command. It will enlarge the active so that it fills the entire screen area. To get the same effect with the mouse you click on the maximise button. I recommend that when you are using CorelDRAW you always have the screen maximised. You can return the window to its previous size by using the Restore command, above, or by clicking on the Maximise button a second time.

Close This command will terminate the current application and return you to the Program Manager. Alternatively you can press **Alt-F4**. There is no mouse equivalent to the command. If you try to close an application that contains a data file, e.g. a graphic, that has not been saved since it was last changed, you will be prompted about saving the file before the program terminates.

Switch To This is a part of Windows 3 that did not exist on previous versions of the program. It allows you to switch from one program to another, provided it is open, quickly and easily without having to reduce everything to an icon first. A shortcut to reach the dialogue box is to use **Ctrl-Esc**. The command pops-up a dialogue box that contains a number of sub-commands.

Switch To allows you to move directly to the selected program. Select the program by clicking on it or use the cursor keys. If the program exists as an icon it will be restored to a window of the size it was before it was reduced to an icon.

End Task will allow you to terminate the selected program. Again you will be prompted about saving any changed file before the program is shut down.

Cancel simply removes the dialogue box from the screen, i.e. it cancels the original command. The shortcut in this case is **Esc** - notice that none of the command letters are underlined.

Cascade will arrange all of the open windows on the screen so that they lie one in front of the other with only their Title Bars visible - just as the Cascade command in the Program Manager arranges sub-windows. The command has no effect on icons.

Tile arranges the open windows so that each occupies roughly the same amount of screen area as the others. Again, the command has no effect on icons.

Arrange Icons will align the icons, i.e. those programs which have been minimised, along the bottom of the screen into a nice, neat row.

Immediately adjacent to the Control Box is the Title Bar. This contains the name of the program, e.g. CorelDRAW, and the name of the file that you are currently using. When you first run CorelDRAW this will say UNTITLED.CDR - in other words the file has not yet been saved and so has no name.

At the left of the Title Bar are two buttons. The first contains a downwards pointing arrow and this is the Minimise switch. Clicking on this will reduce the window to an icon. The second button is the Maximise switch and it contains an upwards pointing arrow. Clicking on this will enlarge the window so that it fills the entire screen. Once you do so the arrow will change into a double headed one. If you now click on this the window will be restored to its former size and shape.

The second line of all Windows applications is the Menu Bar. This contains a list of the main menus of the program and only the first two are common to all windows applications. These are **File** and **Edit**. The former is concerned with inputting and outputting files, e.g. loading a saved file, saving a file, printing a file, importing or exporting elements of a file, etc. The actual commands that the menu will contain depends on applications. The File menu can be activated by pressing **Alt-F** or by clicking on it. To use any of the commands you then press the underlined letter of the command you want.

The commands in all File menus are as follows:

Open This allows you to load a previously saved file into the current application. The command will pop-up a dialogue box that allows you to select a file from anywhere on your hard disk. Double clicking on the filename will load the file into the application for you.

Save Use this command to save the current file to the filename shown on the Title Bar. If you try to use the command with an untitled file you will be prompted to supply a filename.

Save As This will allow you to save the current file to a filename other than the one shown on the Title Bar. In many Windows applications it can also be used to save the file in alternative formats.

Print Does just that - it will send the current file to your printer, normally via the Print Manager, and then allow you to get on with changing the file or using a new one.

Exit This command can be used, in place of the command in the Control box, to terminate the current application and return you to the Program Manager. On some applications the command is called **Quit**.

The Edit menu is concerned, primarily, with the use of the Clipboard. To open the menu either press **Alt-E** or click on the word **Edit** and then press the underlined letter of the command you wish to use. It will contain the following common commands, plus those that are specific to the application itself:

Undo This does exactly what it says - it allows you to cancel an operation and return to a previous condition. For example, you may have moved a part of the graphic you are working on in the wrong direction but you have fixed it in place before you noticed. By using Undo the movement and placement is cancelled and the part of the graphic you moved will be returned to it previous position. Certain Windows applications can go further than this though and the command changes to reflect what you have just done, e.g. it may say Undo Move, Undo Typing, etc. The keyboard shortcut is **Alt-Backspace**.

One of the fundamental parts of the Windows environment is the Clipboard. This is a sub-program that is used to store selected data ready for inserting into other programs or back into the originating program. The following three commands are those which allow you access to the Clipboard from any Windows applications. Before you can place data into the Clipboard you must select it in some way, e.g. by using the mouse, until you do so the commands in the menu will be greyed, i.e. inoperable.

Cut This will copy the selected data from the file into the Clipboard and then delete it from the originating document.

Copy This command is similar to the above but it does not remove the selected data from the original file, i.e. it simply duplicates the data in the Clipboard.

Paste This command is the complement of both the above. It allows you to insert whatever is in the Clipboard into the current file. How it does this depends on the application concerned. In a word processor, for example, the Clipboard contents will be pasted at the cursor position; in CorelDRAW the Clipboard contents will be pasted back wherever they came from originally - assuming that they came from CorelDRAW in the first place.

The final element that is common to the majority of Windows applications are the Scroll Bars. These appear at the left hand side and the base of the window and they allow you to page through the document by fixed increments. Each Scroll bar contains two arrowheads, one at either end, plus a small square which will be positioned somewhere on the bar. You can move the document in a variety of ways depending on how you use the scroll bars themselves.

Click on either arrowhead on the scroll bar and the document will move in that direction by roughly a single line or half an inch, which depends on the type of application. For example, in CorelDRAW when you click on the upwards pointing arrowhead at the top of the left hand scroll bar the page will move upwards by half an inch or 1 cm, depending on which measurement system you are using.

Click on the scroll bar itself and the document moves by a much greater amount. The direction that the document moves will depend on whether you click above or below the little square box on the scroll bar.

Finally you can pick up the little square and move it independently of the fixed increments, provided you use a mouse. Click on the little square and then, while still holding down the mouse button, drag the box in the direction you want the document to move. This allows very fast repositioning of the document but you may well find that the amount you move is so large that you cannot then find your correct place. Using this method works well if you are using text documents, e.g. a word processing file, but it is not recommended if you are using CorelDRAW.

Windows 3 is too large and powerful to be dealt with in depth here. If you want to know more about it and get the best from it then I suggest you get hold of a good book about it.

Chapter 9 Hard Disk Utilities

Disk Utilities

A hard disk supplies you with a large amount of storage space but it should not be treated as just a bin to dump files into. The disk must be organised properly, the files kept in order, old data disposed of, etc. In addition to all this, there are a number of housekeeping tasks that will need to be performed and these are done by utility programs. There are an almost infinite number of utility programs available, ranging from the simple to the exceedingly complex. (On the disk that has been prepared to accompany this book you will find a number of utilities and housekeeping programs, all of them Shareware, along with details of each one.)

Anyone who is using or contemplating using a hard disk should have a certain number of utilities as a matter of course. It is not possible to examine every utility program available - that would take a couple of large volumes which is not practical at the moment - and so in the following sections we are only going to look at the most readily available, and some would say best, of the commercial programs, Norton Utilities, SpinRite and PC Tools. Each of these programs is available from any good dealer or computer shop. We strongly recommend that you purchase, and use, at least one of them, preferably all three.

Norton Utilities

Mention hard disk utilities to anyone and ask them to name a couple of such programs and you can guarantee that one of them will be Norton Utilities. Peter Norton, the guy who created the now famous software, was a journalist who wanted to do things with his computer that just were not possible. So he set about writing a utility to do it. From this small beginning there was no turning back. Peter Norton Computing is, today, one of the major forces in the industry.

Over the years Norton Utilities has grown from those couple of home grown utilities to what amounts to almost an industry standard. Unlike other utilities, Norton is not a single catch-all program instead it is a complete suite of related programs. These can be run individually or from a menu driven front end. The suite consists of 26 distinct utilities - some more useful than others, but all of them are likely to be used at one time or another. Rather than give descriptive details of each one, which would almost require a book by itself, we are only going look briefly at the majority of them concentrating on the ones that are the most useful.

The manuals that accompany the software are superb. The main one, which covers the utilities in detail, provides stacks of information about using the programs and their effects. The second book, the Norton Trouble Shooter, contains a host of details about problem solving with hard disks. The final book, Norton Disk Companion, contains facts and details about hard disks in general. If you intend purchasing a set of utility programs then Norton, preferably the Advanced Edition, should be at the top of your list.

Batch Enhancer

MS-DOS batch files can be extremely powerful but no-one would call them interesting to watch. By their very nature the batch files operate behind the scenes, for all that you can make them display indicative messages of their progress. However, by using the Batch Enhancer you can now make your files all singing, all dancing. The program allows you to add a whole range of enhancements from windows, to sound, to sized characters, to full interactivity. If you like snazzy batch files then this is the program for you.

Disk Information

This one provides you with technical information about the hard disk. This is similar to, but more informative than, the information displayed by the main program, e.g.

```
DI-Disk Information, Advanced Edition 4.50,
(C) Copr 1987-88, Peter Norton

Info from DOS Drive C: Info from boot
record

              system id        'MSDOS3.3'
         media descriptor (hex)         F8
2             drive number
1,024      bytes per sector          1,024
4         sectors per cluster            4
2           number of FATs               2
512     root directory entries         512
```

21	sectors per FAT	21
10,353	number of clusters	
	number of sectors	41,471
1	offset to FAT	1
43	offset to directory	
59	offset to data	
	sectors per track	17
	sides	5
	hidden sectors	17

The information is normally displayed directly to the screen but it can also be redirected to a file - as was done for the illustration above.

System ID - the operating system under which the drive is running.

Media Descriptor - tells you what type of drive it is. The possible values, which are Hexadecimal numbers, are:

F0	1.44 Mb 3.5-inch floppy
F8	A hard Disk, without any distinction to encoding procedure.
F9	1.2 5.25-inch floppy or 720 Kb 3.5-inch floppy
FD	360 Kb 5.25-inch floppy
FE	160 Kb 5.25-inch floppy
FF	320 Kb 5.25-inch floppy

Drive Number - these start at 0 for the one designated A, 1 is Drive-B, 2 is Drive-C, etc.

Bytes per Sector - is self explanatory.

Sectors per Cluster - is the minimum storage unit used by the disk, in this case 4 Kb.

Number of FATs - with all hard disk this will be 2, a RAM-Drive may give a value of 1.

Root Directory Entries - generally all hard disks allow 512 entries, either files or sub-directories, in the root.

Sectors per FAT - the size of the FAT.

Number of Clusters - the amount of storage can be ascertained from this. It also gives an indication of the FAT type. Disks with less than 4085 FAT entries tend to use 12-Bit entries, while those with more than this use 16-bit entries.

Number of Sectors - self explanatory.

Offset to FAT - give the sector number at which the primary FAT is located.

Offset to Directory - the sector number at which the root directory is located.

Offset to Data - where data storage begins.

Sectors per Track - theoretically the number of sectors per track. In this case it is wrong because my disk is RLL encoded and used 26 sectors per track but it is masked to behave as an MFM for reasons that need not be gone into here.

Sides - self explanatory

Hidden Sectors - the starting sector for the MS-DOS partition.

Directory Sort

Allows you to sort the directories and files on your disk into a number of orders, including the files in sub-directories, based on Name, Extension, Date, Time or Size. The program can be used in command line mode and as such, I include it in my AUTOEXEC.BAT, so the disk is always in alphabetical order. The program is extremely useful because it will allow you to order files and directories very quickly which makes finding a particular file or group of files easy and simple.

Disk Test

Is similar to the MS-DOS CHKDSK command but much more extensive because it actually examines the disk rather than just what MS-DOS has to say about it. The program checks for physical damage to the disk, it marks bad sectors and moves any data from such areas to a safe portion of the disk - all automatically. As the program runs it presents you with a running commentary of its activity. Once it has finished you are presented with a report of your disk's performance:

DT-Disk Test, Advanced Edition 4.50,
(C) Copr 1987-88, Peter Norton

Select DISK test, FILE test, or BOTH
Press D, F, or B... D

During the scan of the disk,
you may press BREAK (Control-C)
to interrupt Disk Test

Test reading disk C:, system area and data area

The system area consists of boot, FAT, and directory

No errors reading system area

The data area consists of clusters numbered 2 - 10,354

No errors reading data area

From this it can be seen that this particular disk is exceedingly healthy.

File Attributes

Can be used to display the attributes of the files in any portion of the disk. It can also be used to change those attributes in a similar way to using MS-DOS ATTRIB - the difference being that you can use this program to access all the files on your disk, including those in sub-directories.

File Date/Time

Allows you to change the Date and Time stamping of files - something that you cannot do from MS-DOS.

File Find

One problem that tends to occur with hard disks, and becomes more acute as you increase the total amount of storage space available, is finding a file which you know exists but you cannot remember where you put it. This program solves the problem. It can be used to find any file on any logical or physical drive. All you need to do is supply the filename and the program does the rest. When it finally finds the file, providing it actually exists, it tells you the location, size and Date and Time stamping of the target file. You can also use the wildcard characters if you are unsure of the name - in this case you also get a list of all the directories which match your input.

File Info

For reasons that need not be gone into here, MS-DOS will only allow you to use 8 characters for a filename and another 3 for the extension. This can be a real nuisance at times, especially when compared to the naming of files on Apple machines for example. The hassle of naming files descriptively, but without using the same filename twice can be extremely taxing. However, you can now use this program to remedy the situation. The program allows you to append descriptive detail to any file or directory. The comments are then stored in a file called FILEINFO.FI.

Format Recover

The MS-DOS FORMAT command is destructive to any data that the disk so processed contained. If you should accidentally format your hard disk you are likely to find yourself in deep trouble as a result. The program can be used in a number of modes of which the fail-safe one is probably the most common.

You can use the program as a command line, i.e. FR/SAVE, and include this within your AUTOEXEC.BAT. Then every time that you boot the machine, the program will map your hard disk and save the resulting information. Then, if the disk is accidentally formatted the program can use this file to recover ALL the data, including the directories and all the files they contained. However, even if you have not run the program in fail-safe mode it can still be used to undo the formatting but it becomes a much longer.

File Size

How many times have you wanted to copy a group of files from your hard disk to a floppy and in the process you get a message saying Disk Full or the equivalent? You need never experience it again thanks to this little program. It is used to display the sizes, both apparent and actual, of files - along with the total space required to contain them. Once you have the information, you know whether or not they will fit onto the target disk - the program even makes allowances for the different cluster sizes on dissimilar disks.

List Directories

Gives you a listing, similar to the MS-DOS TREE command, of all the directories and sub-directories on your disk. The program can present the same information in a graphical format which resembles a genealogical tree, so you can see at a glance what is where. Again, you can save this information to a file rather than have it displayed on the monitor.

Line Print

Allows you to send textual files to a printer. So what's special about that? Well, the program allows you to format the printed output by specifying the Top and Bottom margins, the Left and Right margins, the page width, height, line spacing, page numbers and, if you wish, line numbering. You can also include a Header and print files that are not pure ASCII, e.g. those from WordStar.

Norton Control Centre

This program allows you to set a wide range of hardware defaults, e.g. the display colour. You can change the cursor size, the screen or palette colours, the video mode, keyboard rate, serial port specifications, any one of 4 separate clocks and the Time and Date. All this is then stored in a file so that it is always available to you.

Norton Change Directory

Rather than having to input the full path to any directory, you can use this program to move there in a blink of the eye. As you activate the program it presents the directory structure as a graphical image. You then move the highlighter to the directory you want to move to and press Enter. That's it. Much quicker than using MS-DOS.

Norton Disk Doctor

One of the most useful programs in the entire suite. Norton Disk Doctor has saved more data than we care to think about. One of the most common problems is a computer that will not boot from its hard disk. There is one particular make of computer that seems to suffer from this problem more than any other. For some reason the computer seems able to lose its boot sector on a regular basis. Some computers seem more prone to this fault than others.

Before the arrival of Norton Disk Doctor, there was only one cure - make a complete backup of all the data on Drive-C and then do a complete reformat, usually a high level would be sufficient, but sometimes a low level would be required as well. The release of this program helped tremendously. The more knowledgeable reader will have already realised that the problem with the drive was fairly simple, the sectors containing IO.SYS, MSDOS.SYS and COMMAND.COM had become corrupted, for whatever reason. While the problem is fairly simple the solution isn't.

Most people would say that SYS.COM, a MS-DOS supplied utility, is designed to make a disk bootable by transferring the boot sectors, i.e. IO.SYS and MSDOS.SYS to the target disk. You can't simply copy them because they are both hidden, and write protected files that won't respond to the COPY command. SYS.COM will only do this if there is space on the target disk in the right place. This usually means that the disk has only been formatted and no other information has been written to it. SYS.COM does not transfer COMMAND.COM either, this has to be done with a copy command. Unfortunately SYS wouldn't work, every time it was tried it would respond with the message, **No room for system on destination drive**. The only way round that is either reformat or don't try and boot off the drive!

Norton Disk Doctor changed all that! It has a menu option: Make A Disk Bootable. When this option is selected, it will look for the system files and replace them, if it needs to move other software out of the way so that the system files are in the right place, it can do it! The only restriction on its use is that there must be enough room on the target drive for the system files and COMMAND.COM, depending on the version of MS-DOS this will be about 70 or 80 Kb.

That is only one feature of Disk Doctor. The others are:

Recover from DOS's RECOVER

The MS-DOS RECOVER is fairly destructive to files - in fact it should never be used. But if it has been then this option of the Disk Doctor will remedy much of the damage.

Revive a Defective Diskette

This option can be used to repair the damage to files on a floppy disk which has been damaged. The success rate is fairly high but it does depend on the extent of the damage in the first place.

Analyse Disk

This program will carry out a variety of tests on the disk, all of which are non-destructive.

Norton Integrator

This is a menu driven front end program which allows you to run any of the other Norton Utility suite programs. It provides you with brief details of each program in the suite along with a note of the main switches which can be used with each. Having selected a program, adding whatever operands you deem necessary, simply pressing Enter will activate it and shove NI into the background. This then returns, once the program you have selected completes its operation.

Norton Utility

This is the heart of the whole suite. Rather than ask what can it do, you are better off asking what it cannot do. The answer would be it cannot draw a map of the U.K. but it can do just about anything else, especially if it is to do with disks or files. Basically the program allows you to explore any portion of your disk, including the system areas, and then make changes there. The program is menu driven (it needs to be) and when loaded it presents you with three options, each of which contains sub-options:

Explore Disk

Choose Item - brings up a further series of sub-commands that allow you to select a File, Cluster, Sector or Absolute Sector.

Information of Item - presents you with detailed information about the item previously selected.

Edit/Display Item - yields descriptive detail about the item or allows you to select a file from within a directory if you have not already done so. To edit a file for instance you can use either ASCII format, which is simpler but essentially difficult, or Hexadecimal which is neater but requires more thought.

Search Item - allows you to scan through the chosen item to find a specific string of characters.

Write Item - permits you to write the chosen and edited item back to the disk in a number of different modes.

Unerase

Allows you to reinstate any file that might have been accidentally deleted. From the menu you can log onto alternative drives and then select a deleted to unerase.

Disk Information

Map Disk Usage - gives you a graphical image of which areas of the disk are being used. Each square represents a number of clusters but it does provide an overall indication of where the files are and how well organised your disk is.

Technical Information

Gives you basic information about the maximum capacity and how much of it is free, sector sizes, Tracks, etc.

Quick Unerase

Rather than having to go through the procedure with the previous program to recover a file, you can use this one instead - but only if the disk being used has not had additional files written to it since the erasure occurred. The program makes use of the information stored in the file prepared by Format Recover if possible but it can also reinstate files directly from the disk. If you try to redeem a file you will either get it back in its entirety or not at all. If you then want to recover partial files, i.e. some of the original file space has already been allocated to new files, you will have to use Norton Utility itself, as this is the only program that allows you access directly to sectors.

Speed Disk

One of the things that is likely to slow down your disk access time, even on the fastest disk, is file scattering. This happens because of the way in which MS-DOS stores files. When you use a brand new disk, or one that has just been formatted, there is no problem. The files are written to the disk in sequence, each one separately and in its own group of clusters. Such a file is called contiguous.

However take one of those files and load it into a word processor for example, make changes to it and increase its size and then save it again. MS-DOS will fit as much of the file as possible back into the original contiguous clusters but the balance of the file will be placed into the next free cluster. If the remainder of the file will not fit completely then only part of it is stored there and the rest is placed into the next set of available clusters. This process continues until the entire file is written to the disk. You do not notice anything special because the process happens so quickly. The next time you change the file, the process is repeated and so on. Eventually you can get to the point where the file is scattered over every platter and in radically different tracks. Such a file is non-contiguous or fragmented. When you then load the file again MS-DOS and the controller have to work much harder than they should in order to retrieve the data and this slows down the access time.

Speed Disk will solve the problem for you. Quite simply, the program rearranges your disk so that all the files it contains are in contiguous sectors. Ideally you should run the program once a day, say at the end of your working period, so that the files are always at their optimum. The first time you run the program it takes a long time, especially if you have been using the disk for some time and have a large number of fragmented files on it. However, subsequent runs of the program are much faster and if you run it daily it will take less than a minute each time.

Safe Format

As we have said, the MS-DOS FORMAT program is inherently destructive. This is especially true on Compaq machines, and some others, which use a special format routine which actually writes data to the disk as it is formatted. Normally, any data that existed on the disk prior to it being formatted will be lost forever as a result of the formatting process. However, this program in the Norton Utilities suite can be installed in place of the MS-DOS command, which will be renamed to

XXFORMAT.EXE, and used in its place. I will allow you to use one of four differen modes ranging from Safe, which preserve existing data and is extremely fast, to Complet which will try to recover bad sectors. Th program is menu driven and allows you t select a range of options and possibilities. can be used in exactly the same way as MS DOS FORMAT to produce a range of differen capacities and densities.

System Information

Carries out a number of tests on your hardwar and then produces a comparative report, agains an IBM PC or XT, of your system and its disk e.g.

SI-System Information, Advanced Editio 4.50,
(C) Copr 1987-88, Peter Norton

Computer Name: IBM AT
Operating System: DOS 3.30
Built-in BIOS dated: Monday, 22 May 1989
Main Processor: Intel 80386
Serial Ports: 1
Co-Processor: None
Parallel Ports: 1
Video Display Adapter: Vide Graphics Array (VGA)
Current Video Mode: Text, 80 x 25 Colo
Available Disk Drives: 3, A: - C:

DOS reports 640 K-bytes of memory:
136 K-bytes used by DOS and residen programs

504 K-bytes available for application programs

A search for active memory finds:
640 K-bytes main memory (at hex 00000-0A000)
32 K-bytes display memory (at hex 0B800-0C000)
384 K-bytes extended memory (at hex 10000-16000)
ROM-BIOS Extensions found at hex paragraphs: C000

Computing Index (CI), relative to IBM/XT: 16.2
Disk Index (DI), relative to IBM/XT: 5.0

Performance Index (PI), relative to IBM/XT: 12.4

The computer name is actually the emulation that the tested machine is running under, not its manufacturer's name. For example, in this case the machine tested is a Tandon 80386 AT not an IBM AT as stated. The final comparative figures are a measure of the machine's performance only. Useful if you are considering purchasing a new machine and you can obtain the comparison figures for these as they will allow you to judge relative performance of the different machines, however the figures should not be taken as gospel. Equally the disk index only checks Track 0 not the entire disk.

Time Mark

This program will report the current time and date, as read from the battery backed RAM, in a more sensible format than MS-DOS can do, e.g. 4:47 p.m., Tuesday, 23 January 1990. In addition you can use it as a stopwatch using any one of four different clocks.

Text Search

Allows you to search any file, or group of files, for a match to your input string. For example TS *.* [name] /S will search through every file on your hard disk to find a match for [name]. As it finds a match it displays it on screen and tells you;

The Path and filename,
Where in the file the match occurs,
Where the relevant sector is to be found on the disk,
A section of the file and the match, in inverse video.

It also asks if you want to continue the search. Note that the search is not context sensitive. In other words if you were to ask it to find ARCH, it would find every occurrence of that word even if it is embedded in other words, e.g. seARCH, mARCH, ARCHive, hierARCHical, etc. The default search is also not case sensitive, i.e. ARCH, Arch and arch are all identical. However, you can impose a switch on the command to make it so.

Unremove Directory

MS-DOS provides command for creating, moving through and deleting sub-directories and everyone is familiar with them. However, a directory acts as a special type of file, which is why you can only have 512 files or directories in the root but an unlimited number of files in a sub-directory, which contains ordinary files. When you delete a directory you cannot then reinstate any of the files it contained, because they are one level deeper, as it were. Using Norton Utilities itself you can resurrect these files by assembling them sector by sector but it is much easier to use this program. All it does is reinstate deleted directories. Once you have done that you can then run Quick Unerase, see above, and restore the files. It sounds quite minor but it can be one of the most useful programs in the entire suite.

Volume Label

This program allows you to apply, change or delete a label from any disk in much the same way as MS-DOS LABEL does. But this program will also allow you to use lower case letters - something that MS-DOS will not allow.

Wipedisk

WARNING: Do not use this program unless you want to lose all the data permanently.

Confidentiality of data on a computer system is almost impossible to guarantee and the British Government's recent efforts to outlaw hacking are not going to make any difference.

A computer system is, by definition, open to abuse and therefore the data it contains is always susceptible to exploitation and/or violation. There are a number of utility programs that will allow you to encrypt data but as they are written by people they can be broken by people. However, if you want to make a disk, either hard or floppy, totally irrecoverable you can use this program.

It overwrites every sector on the disk, rather than just deleting the files, with specific characters. You can even select to use one or more of the cryptograms developed by the US Department of Defence! The program can be run on selected parts of a disk or the entire thing and it has a number of fail safes built into it which mean that it cannot be run accidentally. If you do decide to run it you will find that it takes a long time, depending on the options you select, e.g. a 1.2 Mb floppy may take anything up to 15 minutes to completely wipe even at its simplest level.

Wipefile

WARNING: Do not use this program unless you want to lose the data permanently.

Uses the same kind of techniques as the previous program but it applies them to specific files only - not the entire disk. As with the previous program, once it has been run there is absolutely no way that the files can be recovered.

SpinRite II

Unlike Norton Utilities or PC Tools, SpinRite is a specialist program. Its purpose is to maintain and restore the actual hard disks. The program, which costs around £70 and is completely self-contained and provides you with a multitude of information about your hard disk in a way that no other program does. SpinRite is primarily meant to allow you to reformat the hard disk sector by sector - without having to remove the data that is contained in the sectors first. It will also allow you to optimise the sector interleaving, recover data which has been placed into defective sectors and repair damaged sectors. There are very few utility programs that we would consider absolutely vital and essential for hard disk use, and SpinRite is one of them. If you own a hard disk, you should definitely purchase a copy of this program.

Originally released in the mid 1980's, the program has been enhanced and improved considerably, incorporating many qualities that users of the original wanted to see. Gibson Research, who created the program, are one of the very few, you can count them on one hand, companies in the computer industry who actually listen to the users and try to give them what they ask for. That process continues today; you can ring up the company and tell them what you like about the program and what you would like to see changed. If enough people ask for the same thing then the next version of the program will incorporate those features. In addition, you receive unlimited technical support for the program.

The program will work with any disk that uses MFM, RLL or ERLL encoding. Amongst its current features are the following:

The ability to low level format a disk running under MS-DOS while that disk is in use, i.e. the data does not have to be removed from the disk first. It does this by reading the data from a single sector and placing it into the memory, then reformatting that sector before replacing the data. It then moves onto the next sector and repeats the process. Of necessity this takes a long time - usually about 8 hours for a 32 Mb disk - but seeing as the program is self contained you can run this element overnight. The reason for reformatting like this is simply to improve the disk performance and to protect against creeping sector errors. At the same time, the program can optimise the Interleave Factor, providing you have asked it to, by allowing for all the components of the drive and controller to give you the best possible performance. In the process of reformatting, SpinRite can recover sectors that have gone bad and return them to active use.

Data Pattern testing is used to check the individual sectors. The program carries out 82 extensive tests on each sector. This means that on a 32 Mb drive the program will write, verify and read more than 5 Gb of data in total to ensure the disk works correctly. In effect, the program scrubs the disk clean and so ensures that the disk will always be readable after this operation. If a sector proves to be on the point of collapse and cannot be recovered then the data it contains will be moved to a safe area to prevent loss. Again this process takes a long time, 7 to 8 hours for a 32 Mb disk, and is best run overnight. It is possible to combine this pattern testing with the reformatting process so that the two are performed in conjunction if they are combined then the whole process takes about 10 hours on a 32 Mb disk. Separate tests are used for each coding technology used.

Recover unreadable data using purpose written diagnostic routines, which can bypass the controller if necessary, to recover the data. SpinRite can recover files that no other program, even Norton, can salvage.

The Quick surface scan, which takes only minutes to run, can help pin-point any sector that may be on the point of collapse, thus giving you adequate warning of possible problems.

Report generation is an automatic process. Every time you run the program the results are added to a text file, stored in the root of the drive being tested, so that you have a complete commentary covering each test. In actuality the program only stores the last 1,000 lines of the report but that is enough to record some 30 to 40 runs of SpinRite.

SpinRite is menu driven which makes it very simple and easy to use. Each menu screen also contains a dialogue box which gives brief details of the currently highlighted command. Once the program has been loaded, you are presented with a choice of 6 possible functions ranging from Quick Surface Scan to Quit. You can also change the way the program works, print a summary of the program's operation or display detailed information about the program. It is certainly one of the best and most user-friendly menu screens we have ever seen. In fact, the opening screen sums up the whole approach of Gibson Research - treat people as people and not as faceless users. It certainly makes a refreshing change.

Using the program

The nice thing about SpinRite is that it requires no esoteric foreknowledge as it is run it will provide you with information about what it is doing and why. For example, the Quick Surface Scan, which should be run the first time you use the program, checks each of the following areas and the dialogue box across the bottom of the screen tells you why. Combining this with the manual, you can very quickly acquire an awful lot of knowledge about hard disks and how they work.

Checking System RAM

Because of the way it works, SpinRite requires that you do not have any memory resident programs loaded - SpinRite needs the memory and must have a sufficient amount of it to work properly. This does not apply to partition drivers like that used by Disk Manager. Equally the program cannot be used on a network or with a multi-tasking system.

Checking Disk Controller

This ensures that the controller is working correctly. A fault here could mean something as simple as the cables being connected incorrectly, or it could point to a serious error on the controller itself.

Checking Controller RAM

As above.

Checking for Disk Caching

Again, this uses memory which SpinRite may require to operate correctly. You are better off disabling any disk cache while running the program.

Checking Partition Mapping

SpinRite can only operate with up to 8 partitions on one physical drive.

Once the program completes the above diagnostics it then performs the surface scan. Each track and sector is checked and tested to verify its condition - the process takes about 4 minutes for a 32 Mb disk, depending on type. As the test is run, you get a graphical representation of its progress or you can switch to the Technical Log or Sector Summary. The surface scan writes and verifies the maximum number of bytes that the disk can contain.

When the surface scan is completed you can return to the main menu and then run the Analysis section of SpinRite. This is the heart of the program. This again checks the system elements mentioned above before beginning the true analysis which is a number of distinct operations.

Performance Evaluation

Checks the Track-to-Track time, the time taken for a full stroke, and finally the time taken for a random seek operation. This last element uses 1,000 tests to get an average figure, with the result that the times shown are very accurate.

System Parameters

Gives a true measure of the disk's rotational speed. This works perfectly with MFM disks but for some reason, appears to be wrong with RLL or ERLL disk, and frequently gives times that are anything up to 600 RPM slower than they should be! In addition, it gives details of the number of bits per track, the inter-sector angle, the encoding being used and the controller interface, the data transfer rate and the current interleave. All of this is purely for your information, as SpinRite handles all reformatting parameters automatically.

At the end of this test, the program will tell you if the disk can be reformatted. Some disks cannot be reformatted, in particular those that use ERLL encoding. For example, the disk drive in the Tandon machine that this is being written on uses ERLL encoding but it is disguised as MFM. This means that the system thinks it is using MFM encoding, and even Norton confirms this, with its 17 sectors per track when it is actually using 26 sectors. Because of this, SpinRite cannot pattern test the disk but it can still reformat it.

Interleave Performance

SpinRite checks the current interleave factor and displays the transfer rate it provides. It then tests and shows the effects of using alternative interleaves, ranging from 1:1 to 8:1. Once this is done you can select an alternative factor if you wish. Generally though, you are likely to find that the current interleave is correct - but not always.

Reformatting

Before selecting this you can choose the level of pattern testing that will be used. If you are using the program for the first time then you should designate Thorough Testing, which will perform the most comprehensive series of tests your disk is ever likely to encounter. If you have used the program previously then you can use a less extensive testing regime. The depth of testing will affect the time taken for the process, ranging from 7 hours for the heaviest test to minutes for shallow testing. As this test runs you again get the graphical representation of it. Alternatively, you can blank the screen while the test runs.

Ideally, you should run SpinRite at its simplest level about once a week and at the thorough level every couple of months to ensure that your disk achieves optimum performance. The software is not copy protected and so it can be installed on any system by simply copying the master disks. As well as the software, you get a comprehensive manual and a booklet about hard disks in general - both of which contain a wealth of information. Each is written in a light, conversational style that makes them easy to read and understand.

SpinRite is certainly one of the most useful utility programs we have ever encountered and it is difficult to contain our enthusiasm for it. If you have a hard disk then we strongly recommend that you purchase a copy of the program - it could well be the most important piece of software you ever buy.

PC Tools

PC Tools was originally released in 1985 and since then it has undergone a number of updates, expansions and rewrites until today the latest is Version 7.1, however the following information is based on Version 4.3. The program is very similar to Norton Utilities but instead of having a number of related subprograms, PC Tools uses a single main program which provides all of the main utilities, accessed from a front-end menu. In addition, there are five related programs which operate independently and are run directly from the system prompt;

COMPRESS - a file unfragmenter and disk organiser
MIRROR - similar to Norton Format Recover
PCBACKUP - for making security copies of data files
PCRESTOR - the complement to the above
REBUILD - the complement of MIRROR

When you run PC Tools you are presented with an opening screen that gives you the option of using the File Functions, by pressing any key, or the Disk functions, by pressing F3. Because the program provides roughly the same capabilities as Norton, which we have already covered, we are only going to look briefly at both of these but we will concentrate on the related programs. One disadvantage of PC Tools is that it does not provide on-line help of any sort - merely a list of keystrokes. To use the program properly, especially if you are a beginner, you must have the manual available or you will quickly get lost in the program's complexities.

The File Functions

Once selected, you are presented with a menu type screen that contains a list of the files in the current sub-directory, including all their attributes, with the highlighter overlaying the first of these. Moving the highlighter and pressing Enter places a numeral at the start of each file, i.e. before the filename, and this is the order in which the files will be processed by the sub-commands. These are shown along the bottom of the screen and comprise the following;

COPY which is identical to the MS-DOS command in action. Once selected you are asked to specify the target drive and then you are presented with a graphical tree of the directories on that drive. Move the highlighter to the one you want and the files are then copied in the order you specified.

MOVE acts in the same way but it deletes the files from the source directory as part of a single operation.

COMP allows you to compare files in one directory with those in another, even on another disk.

FIND is used to scan the selected file to find a string of characters that matches your input. The input can be either in ASCII, which produces a case sensitive search, or in HEX which produces an exact match.

RENAME does just that but allows you to selectively change the filename or the extension.

DELETE removes files but asks for confirmation first.

VER checks that the file is stored correctly, i.e. verifies it on the disk.

VIEW/EDIT allows you to examine the file intimately, in much the same way as Norton Utility. With program files you are shown a block of Hexadecimal values while the left hand side of the screen gives ASCII equivalents. With a text file you are shown the ASCII characters.

ATTRIB allows you to change any of the four file attributes, i.e. Archive, Read Only, Hidden or System, plus the time and date stamping.

WORDP is a text editor and it will allow you to edit any text file. You can carry out a number of editing options, such as search or paste, within the file with ease.

PRINT sends a copy of the file to the printer.

LIST sends a directory listing to the printer.

SORT allows you to resort the listing of files in the directory by Name, Extension, Date or Size. This only affects the display but you have the option of actually rearranging the files on the disk as well.

HELP displays two 'pages' of the available keystrokes and single line definitions of what they do.

With most of the commands, pressing Esc allows you to step back one operation, e.g. you press Move instead of Copy and notice it before the process starts. This key is also used to terminate the program.

Disk and Special Functions

By pressing F3 when the start up screen appears, you are taken directly to the second set of commands that PC Tools possesses. These all relate directly to the disk rather than the files it may contain. As with much of PC Tools, some of the commands are very similar to MS-DOS but they are much more user friendly in that they provide you with prompts before the action is carried out.

COPY can be considered identical to the MS-DOS DISKCOPY, i.e. make an identical copy of a floppy disk. You cannot use the command with hard disks or a Ramdrive.

COMPARE is also for floppy disks only and it checks that the files contained on two disks are identical. Similar to MS-DOS COMP.

FIND will search all the files on a disk to find a character string.

RENAME allows you to change the volume label.

VERIFY does what it says but has the added ability to try and repair data files which may have been damaged.

VIEW/EDIT is identical to the Files command of the same name.

MAP gives a graphical representation of the disk and the files it contains. You can also use the command to map individual files - useful if you think the files are fragmented.

LOCATE is a global find command, i.e. you input a filename and the program then searches the entire disk to try to find a match. If it is successful, you are shown the full path to each such file.

INITIALISE will format a floppy disk.

DIRECTORY MAINTENANCE allows you to add or remove directories, subject to the usual MS-DOS contingencies, or to rename an existing directory. You can also use the command to prune and graft directories - which sounds odd but is very useful. Basically, this option permits you to pick up an entire sub-directory, complete with its contents, and disassociate it from its current parent. You can then move the entire thing and splice it onto another directory and so reorganise your directory tree. This is one command that PC Tools has which Norton does not.

UNDELETE is used to recover deleted files.

SYSTEM INFO presents you with a host of information about your system that is similar to Norton SI. However it is not as extensive and does not check the actual disks for performance.

PARK moves the disk heads to a safe station so that the system can be moved to another location.

Associated Programs

In addition to the menu driven commands of the main program PC Tools comes complete with five other programs that perform special functions. Each one is run directly from the system prompt and provides its own command structure - again though there is little or no on-line help.

COMPRESS

This is the most useful of these and we prefer it to Norton Speed Disk. It does not, as you might think, archive files, instead it is used to unfragment your files and place them all into contiguous clusters. As it moves the files around, the program also arranges them so that the slack space, i.e. the extra part of the cluster that does not contain data, is placed at the end of the contiguous clusters. This speeds up the data transfer rate and makes the entire disk operation cleaner and more precise. As the program is run it displays the opening menu which contains 6 sub-commands, the first and last operate together while the other four are independent. (Do not run Compress if you have FASTOPEN loaded.)

SORT allows the user to specify the order in which the files will be arranged on the disk, e.g. by specifying Ascending Filenames. This option is used in conjunction with the final option only.

DISK ANALYSIS checks the MS-DOS information about the disk and then presents you with a report of its findings, e.g. the number of allocated clusters, the amount free, the number of bad sectors, etc. The command makes no changes to the disk.

FILE ANALYSIS displays a report of how the files are organised on the disk by giving the file or directory name, the number of clusters it uses and if the file is fragmented. Again, the command does not make any changes to the disk, it merely generates a report.

SURFACE ANALYSIS does just that. It checks the entire disk, displaying a graphical map as it does so, and shows which areas are allocated to what. The process takes some time depending on the disk size and the controller being used. You may generate a filed report of the process if you wish.

ORGANISATION ANALYSIS can be run to check whether or not the disk needs to have the final option run on it. The option does not change the disk in any way.

COMPRESSION is the option that makes the changes to the files by unfragmenting them and placing them in contiguous sectors. To run this option you must not have any TSR programs operating because the Compress function requires large amounts of RAM for its operation. You can select one of three compression routines: Minimum compression, Full compression or Complete compression. If you select the latter then the program also scrubs the unused clusters so that they contain no extraneous data.

Once you make your selection the program then runs automatically. If, for any reason, there is a fault with the disk, e.g. lost chains, then the program does not run but it will suggest a course of action that may remedy the situation. The compression can be terminated at any time by pressing Esc but this should be avoided if at all possible.

Once the program has terminated it displays a message about rebooting the machine. Ideally you should do this whenever the disk is compressed.

MIRROR

This can be run directly after the COMPRESS program or separately from the system prompt. Basically it backs up the FAT and Root every time it is run so that in the event of a disk crash you can recover lost data. However to be effective the program must be run daily, e.g. by including it in your AUTOEXEC.BAT. By itself the program is simply a safeguard, in order to recover lost data you have to use the REBUILD program.

PCBACKUP

This is similar to the MS-DOS BACKUP command but it is far superior and much faster. The big advantage to it is that it will format the floppy disks automatically in the process, you just replace the disks as prompted and the program does the rest. In addition, the program allows you to be selective about the files that will be treated - something that is next to impossible with MS-DOS. You can also use the program with any size of floppy. However, as with MS-DOS BACKUP, the security copies of the files cannot be used directly - they must be restored first.

PCRESTOR

This is the complement to PCBACKUP and it is used to replace the backed up files to the hard disk.

REBUILD

This is the final program in the suite and it is the partner of MIRROR. It should only be used in the event of a disastrous disk crash. The program will recreate the FAT and ROOT by using the duplicate copy of these which has been created by MIRROR - any files which have been added or changed since the last time MIRROR was run will not be rebuilt, because as far as this program is concerned they do not exist. However if you have accidentally deleted every file on the disk, e.g. by using DEL *.* or through using FORMAT, then the program can recover the files that it knows about. In this it is similar to Norton Format Recover and Quick Unerase.

PC Tools, and its subprograms, is one of the major utility programs which you can obtain. While it is similar to Norton, the two utilities also contain a range of differences which actually complement each other rather than making them mutually exclusive. Ideally, you should have both utilities and learn to use them. When using a hard disk they should be considered essential.

Chapter 10 Trouble shooting

Common Questions

Below are some of the most common questions that people ask about hard disks, and their answers. Generally speaking these will fall into one of two categories, either about the disk itself or about using it. Most questions can be answered with a little common sense, which unfortunately is not as common as you would think, but the ones below are of a more esoteric nature. The questions are listed roughly in the order that they are asked, the most frequent ones first.

Do I really need a hard disk?

No is the short answer. But a hard disk will make your system more dynamic, responsive and much easier to use. A hard disk provides you with a huge amount of data storage, it allows you very fast access, and it opens up the operating parameters of the system to levels you could only dream about when you were using a floppy based machine. Once you do fit a hard disk you will wonder what you ever did without one. Besides which, much of today's modern software requires a massive amount of storage space to hold the necessary files and only a hard disk can give you this. However if you want to continue struggling along at a snail's pace when your computer could be moving at far better speed then that's your affair....

Can I put this disk into my system?

Providing you are using the correct controller with the drive then yes, you can - within limits. Firstly, most XT's, and quite a few AT's, have only got room to mount three drives within the carrier. So if you are already using two floppy drives and a hard disk then you do not have room, unless you discard one of the drives. On a number of AT's, and not always the higher priced ones, there is room to install more drive units within the machine. So it very much depends on the system you have. External hard drives are rare, with the exception of the Tandon Ad-Pac, and so the vast majority of hard drives must be mounted internally - they need the protection that the system casing gives them and the ability to discharge stray electrical currents safely.

What size disk should I buy?

That's like asking how long is a piece of string? It depends on what you are doing with your computer. If you are running just a word processor and the odd small program then a 32 Mb disk will probably be sufficient. On the other hand if you are running a DTP program, multiple Windows applications, a large spreadsheet and a huge database then you will need much more. Personally, neither of us can manage with less than 70 Mb - in fact one of us uses 120 Mb and will shortly need to increase this. Basically it is horses for courses but you should always buy a disk that is slightly too large for your current needs because you will find you need the extra capacity. But don't be daft about it, don't buy a 300 Mb drive if you think you will only need 32 Mb. Generally you will find that the next size up, say a 60 Mb in place of a 32 Mb, is sufficient.

Can I use the drive sideways?

In other words, can I use it in a tower system? The answer is yes. A hard disk can be installed either horizontally or vertically but it should not be at any other angle. Similarly it should be formatted in the orientation that it will be used in. This latter point is not essential but it helps. Equally if you are going to change the orientation of the drive you should park the heads before you do so.

Can I put an RLL drive into a system containing an MFM one?

Theoretically you can but... It is not a good idea to have two incompatible controllers in the same system. However some controllers will allow you to do so. Check the one you want to use and make sure it will allow you to select the controller address. Generally speaking if you are using MFM or RLL drives you can only have two hard disks in one system because the controller can only handle two drives. Besides which, most systems have only a limited number of power supply cables available. If you need to create an additional supply you must obtain a piece of kit called a Y-splitter. This allows you to make one power cable into two. But don't use too many of them or you will find that you are trying to draw more power than the computer power supply unit can give you. Equally don't put an IDE drive into a system containing an MFM or RLL drive or vice versa. Essentially - Don't mix controllers.

How do I know what drive type this is for the SETUP?

Curiously enough you can't - at least not easily because the drives are not labelled with their types. However you will know the number of Cylinders, Read/Write Heads and Sectors that the drive contains. From this information you can tell what type it is by referring to the drive type list that the SETUP gives you. On the Tandon for example there is a little program called DRIVES.COM that lists the types of drive it allows. By running this program first you can find the type of drive that you want to install, even if it means running the program from a floppy drive. On other machines it is more difficult, try asking the dealer who supplied it. Alternatively ring the disk manufacturer and ask them.

Is my current controller compatible with this drive?

Check the controller manual and find out what interface it uses and then choose the appropriate drive to match. For example all Seagate RLL drives have the suffix R, SCSI drives have N suffix while normal MFM drives have no suffix.

What Interleave Factor do I use?

This depends on a number of factors. Most of the very fast AT machines will use an interleave of 1:1 and the disks come preformatted as that. On others the interleave will be either 2:1 or 3:1; again they will be preformatted to this specification. An XT may use an Interleave of 6:1, or even in exceptional cases of 8:1. Get a copy of SpinRite and use it to check the effects of different Interleaves. The advantage of using SpinRite is that it takes into account the whole system effect rather than just the drive throughput.

Data Security

A hard disk is an electromechanical device and as such it is liable to go wrong eventually. Fortunately major problems with disks are very rare but minor problems are fairly common. There is no guarantee that any disk is fault free, nor can you say that one particular make of disk is more likely to produce faults than another. The major hassle with fault finding on hard disks is that the problem does not necessarily reside on the disk. The most common predicament is caused by the cables not being connected correctly or more simply by someone bashing the disk. A hard disk is a delicate precision instrument, on a par with a high quality record player. You cannot expect this to work correctly if you mistreat it, and the same thing applies to hard disks. They must be treated with care and due attention for what they are. In reality 99.999% of hard disks will provide you with exemplary performance throughout their lives and you will never encounter a single problem or error. On the other hand if a disk does go wrong the problems it causes can be horrendous.

There are a few simple safeguards you can take to offset these - and you can be sure that the one time you neglect to do them, the disk will go wrong.

1) Always back up your data.

This cannot be stressed often enough. This is THE most effective precaution you can take. The strange thing is that everyone knows it but very few people actually practise it. If your disk crashes you can always reinstate the main programs you use simply by reinstalling them, from their copies not the master disks, but the data files are another matter.

Data, by its very nature, is a constantly changing entity. In the course of writing this book for instance each chapter has been chopped and changed, altered, modified or amended six or seven times and that discounts the sub-editing and proofing they receive when they are typeset. Because of this there are always three copies of the files in existence at any one time using a system called Grandfather, Father, Son. (Yes, we know it is sexist but the term derives from long before the feminist movement appeared.)

The method is simple but it provides almost guaranteed data security and it operates like this.

Step 1 - As soon as the data file is created make a backup of it on a floppy disk. This is the Son.

Step 2 - When you change the original make a backup of the altered file onto a second disk. This is now the Son, and the first disk is the Father.

Step 3 - As more changes are made, make a backup of these onto a third floppy. This is now the Son, the floppy from Step 2 becomes the Father and the original copy becomes the Grandfather.

Step 4 - Any further changes are also backed up but always onto the disk that is the

Grandfather which becomes the Son. The other two floppies then advance a generation, i.e. the Father become the Grandfather and the previous Son becomes the Father. The process then continues until the data reaches its final stage of completion.

The only problem with using this system is that it uses a lot of floppy disks and you have to label them very accurately, however the advantages far outweigh both of these problems. The advantage of it is that you always have duplicate copies of the data. Even if the two newest copies should be destroyed for some reason you have not lost everything.

2) Buy some utilities and use them frequently.

At the very least you should have a copy of Norton Utilities, or PC Tools, and SpinRite. In total they will cost you just over £120 but they are worth their weight in gold. So get them, read the associated manuals and learn to use the software. They will save you time, effort, hassle and stop you going grey prematurely or tearing your hair out. Using the utilities will provide you with a better understanding of how your disk works, they will improve your disk's performance and protect your data.

3) Treat your hard disk with respect.

Get into the habit of parking the heads. Do this every time before you power down the system. By parking the heads you move them to a safe area of the disk so that if anyone bashes the system box the heads will not crash into the platters and cause irretrievable damage to both the disk and your data. Always park the heads before moving the system - even if it is only to the other side of your desk.

If your disk has less than roughly 5% of its capacity left free, then either get a new disk or remove extraneous files from it. The majority of today's software will create temporary files on your hard disk as it is used (Windows in particular does this) and these files can be enormous - anything up to 1 Mb each. If there is insufficient room for them then the program will not work properly. Keep your disk tidy and compact and it will perform much better.

4) Only use the disk with its corresponding controller.

You cannot improve the amount of storage you get from an MFM drive by connecting it to an RLL controller. The drive will apparently format to the higher density but then it will begin to deteriorate rapidly. In fact the disk is likely to suffer physical damage. If you do use the wrong controller then you automatically nullify the guarantee that comes with the disk. All hard disks are manufactured to very high standard, much higher than those of a stereo system for instance, but the manufacturers cannot be held responsible for purposeful misuse by the user.

5) If you are doing a lot of disk swapping and/or sharing get Anti-Virus protection.

There are more and more viruses around these days. Certainly since we wrote the first edition of this book, the number of viruses has at least tripled. We strongly recommend that you get some kind of virus protection if you are swapping disks between machines. The Anti-Virus Toolkit from S&S Enterprises is in our view, the best and it costs less than £100.

If you take all of the above steps you will minimise the problems which you will encounter when you do have a disk failure but even if the disk does fail then your data will be safe.

Disk Problems

The list that follows contains most of the errors that you may encounter when using a hard disk. They are not specific to any disk or controller and where feasible we have given a possible solution. However the list should not be taken as complete although it is comprehensive, i.e. we have left out the more obscure and rarest problems. If you cannot repair a fault on your disk then you should contact either your dealer or the manufacturer - both should have technical support people available to help and assist you with problems. Whatever you do NEVER open the Hard Drive Assembly unit and expose the platters and heads to the air.

The Access Time is not as stated

If you run a program like SpinRite it will give you a very accurate measure of the real Access Time of the disk and this may not correspond with the information in the manufacturer's details. The problem arises because different programs measure the Access Time in different ways, for instance SpinRite provides you with three measures. The figures quoted by the disk makers are generally Random Access Time and they are highly accurate. If you run a test program which measures the time in a different way then of course you will get different results. It is like Government mileage figures for a car and the ones you actually get. According to the former my car should do 37 MPG at 30 MPH but seeing as I rarely, if ever, drive at a consistent 30 MPH for that distance my car never returns that figure - albeit that it does give about 35 MPG. Disk speeds are much the same sort of beast and providing you are not getting times which are radically different, e.g. 1 Mb/Sec as opposed to 5 Mb/Sec, then don't worry about it. If the times are of a completely different order of scale then you should get technical support from either the dealer or the manufacturer.

The drive does not work on alternative system

This problem will not occur unless you move the disk to another system and even then it may not appear. Basically, the pairing of the drive and the controller is a symbiotic one. The combination of controller and drive is a unit and when you format the drive you incorporate any foibles that the controller may have. If you then connect the disk to another controller you may find that the disk is no longer usable.

The answer is to remove all the data to backups and then reformat the drive using the new controller. Once that is completed you will find the problem is cured.

The drive will not format

This usually only applies to XT's and it simply means that the low level format has not been done. The program which fails is the high level format, e.g. the MS-DOS command. See Chapter 5 for full details of the low level format and how to do it.

Large amount of bad sectors

It is fairly rare for any disk to be totally free of bad sectors (although the situation improves constantly) as the manufacturers cannot be 100% certain of producing perfect platters. In actuality it is likely that there is only a tiny error on a single sector but MS-DOS deals in Clusters and Tracks and thus you may apparently have more bad sectors than are actually present. Don't worry about it.

Large number of Read/Write errors occurring

If your drive suddenly begins to develop a large number of bad sectors over a course of time, i.e. you have been using the disk for five years or more, then you may need to replace the drive completely. This is due to wear and tear and is unavoidable. When you consider the number of Read/Write operations that a disk carries out every day, let alone over five years, it is not surprising that it begins to deteriorate. However that is not to say that a disk won't last five years - they do. But remember that a current computer generation is somewhere around 28 months, so five years represents over two generations. You can correct the problem by backing up your data and then reformatting the drive from the beginning.

Low level formatting takes a long time

A low level format should take no more than 5 to 10 minutes, even on a very high capacity drive. If it takes longer than this then there is an error somewhere. Check the data cable, i.e. the 20-pin one, and ensure that it is connected properly. On an AT make sure that the cable from Drive 0, i.e. the one containing partition C, is connected to J4 on the controller. Drive 1 should be connected to J3. Make sure that the cables are connected properly on the controller - it is very easy to slot them wrongly and so miss a pair of pins. Similarly check the power supply.

RLL drive does not achieve capacity

Are you sure you are using the correct controller? This problem is only likely to occur if you are using an RLL drive with an MFM controller.

Drive is gradually losing capacity for no reason

This is the hazard of fitting incompatible controllers into the one system, however it does not always occur. Frequently if you add an RLL disk and controller to a system that has previously been using an MFM disk and controller you will find that the original begins to suffer this problem. The only answer is to remove one of the controller and disk combinations. Never put incompatible disks onto the same controller - it will not work for more than a very short period of time.

Numerical Error Messages

1701 - Disk Error or not ready

The first time I saw this I flipped. The disk was running, the light was on so what did it mean Disk not ready? Quite simply it means that the controller is not getting the required response from the hard disk. In other words the drive has failed the POST. The only recourse open to you is to boot the machine from a floppy disk, so you can get the operating system loaded, and then explore further. What you do next depends on what you find.

If the disk is present, i.e. you can log onto it by entering C:, then you should check the connections. Shut down the machine and remove the power, i.e. disconnect it from the mains, and then open the case. Check the ribbon cables are connected - better yet, remove them and then reconnect them. Reboot the machine while the casing is open and the drive is exposed. With luck the disk boots and you no longer have a problem.

If you cannot log onto the disk then it is worth while carrying out the above operation anyway. It might work - in fact it generally does. If necessary replace the cables with new ones and make sure the jump connectors and terminating resistor are properly set. Check the power supply. Then reboot the machine. If you still get the error then you really do have a problem and it could be either the disk or the controller. Now things get complicated because you need to be able to check both independently, i.e. you need a second machine complete with a second controller and a second drive. Because the majority of computer users will not have these facilities you will have to take the drive and controller to a dealer to have it checked.

1702 - Time Out

The drive is not returning a signal to the computer during the POST within the preset interval. Check that the cables are properly connected and that the power leads are correctly aligned. Check also that the disk is spinning, this will involve having the case open so you can both see and hear the central motor. The disk should spin at a consistent rate and it should achieve orbital speed within seconds of power up. Thereafter the disk should spin consistently at speed.

If the disk is not reaching speed, i.e. the central spindle does not appear to be rotating properly, then there is a physical fault in the drive. It should be returned to the dealer and a replacement obtained. Equally if the disk spins, stops and then spins and stops again in a series of random jerks then it is faulty and should be returned.

1703 - Seek Failure

This error will normally occur if the disk has not been low level formatted. If it definitely has been, then the problem probably lies with the controller. Again the disk and controller need to be checked by a dealer.

1704 - Controller Failed

This one is very rare. Check the drive select and the cables. If the error still appears it means that there is a major fault with the controller which needs to be replaced.

1705 - No Record

The data you try to access does not appear on the disk. It is unusual to see this error - generally you will get the MS-DOS error message File not found.

1706 - Write Fault

The system cannot write the data to the disk. This can be caused by all kinds of things, from the simple to the complex. The most probable cause is that there is no longer any room on the disk to store the file and this can occur when the disk is more than 95% full. Try deleting unwanted files and then saving the file you want again. Alternatively save the file to a floppy and then terminate the software you are using. This will also shut down any and all temporary files the software creates. You can then delete a number of old files and, using a utility like PC Tools Compress, make all the existing files contiguous. This will improve the disk performance and make room for the original file. However, if your drive is that full then you need to seriously consider fitting a second or larger drive unit.

1707 - Track 0 Error

Track 0 is the most important one on the disk because it contains Sector 0, which is the one used to boot from the disk. The problem can occur if the disk has not been high level formatted.

I have encountered this error only once, with the additional message that Sector 0 was bad, even though I had been using the disk for some months. No matter what I tried, I could not recover the disk - I tried a new controller and reformatting the disk at all levels, including repartitioning it. Nothing would work and yet I knew that the disk was good because it had been working perfectly. Then, purely by chance, I disconnected the battery backed RAM in the process of refitting the original controller. Lo and behold the disk worked perfectly! With hindsight we were able to discover what had happened.

The particular machine I was using recorded the error messages from the disk in the battery backed RAM and then did not bother to actually check the disk, but always referred to this record. By disconnecting the battery I had forced the computer to actually check the disk - which it found to be perfectly all right. Reconnecting the battery later, effectively reset the battery backed RAM and the problem has not recurred since. End of problem.

The point about this is that it is not necessarily the drive or the controller that goes wrong. It can be the way that the machine and the drive relate to each other. Therefore when you do get an error message you should check every possible contingency before giving up in despair.

1708 - Bad Select Error

Check the control cable, i.e. the 34-pin one. Is it connected properly?

1709 - Bad ECC

This is a controller error and as such you will need to have the controller checked by a dealer.

1710 - Read Buffer Override

Check the Interleave factor. Try running SpinRite or an equivalent utility. If the problem still occurs then the fault probably lies in the controller. Again this requires a visit to the dealer.

1712 - Bad Address Mark

Is the drive low level formatted? This is the most probable cause of the error. If it is, then the fault may lie in the controller.

1714 - Drive Select Error

Check the jumper connectors and the cables. Connect both properly.

1726 - Data Compare Error

Check the drive formatting using Norton Disk Doctor. Use a utility like SpinRite to reformat the drive.

1770 - Surface Errors

As for 1726

1780 - Setup Error Drive 0

Check the data cable, i.e. the 20-pin one, and the power supply of the first drive. This error only occurs when the cable is not properly connected.

1781 - Setup Error Drive 1

Check the data cable and power supply on the second drive.

1782 - Controller Failure

The controller has developed a major fault. Return it to the dealer for testing, although you will probably need to buy a new one.

1790 - Drive 0 Error

Drive-C needs to be formatted. It may be that you have not correctly identified the drive type. Check to make sure.

1791 - Drive 1 Error

Drive-D needs to be formatted.

Index

- A -

- B -

- C -

- D -

- E -

- F -

- G -

- H -

- I -

- J -

- K -

- L -

- M -

- N -

- O -

- P -

- Q -

- R -

- S -

- T -

- U -

- V -

- W -

- X -

- Z -